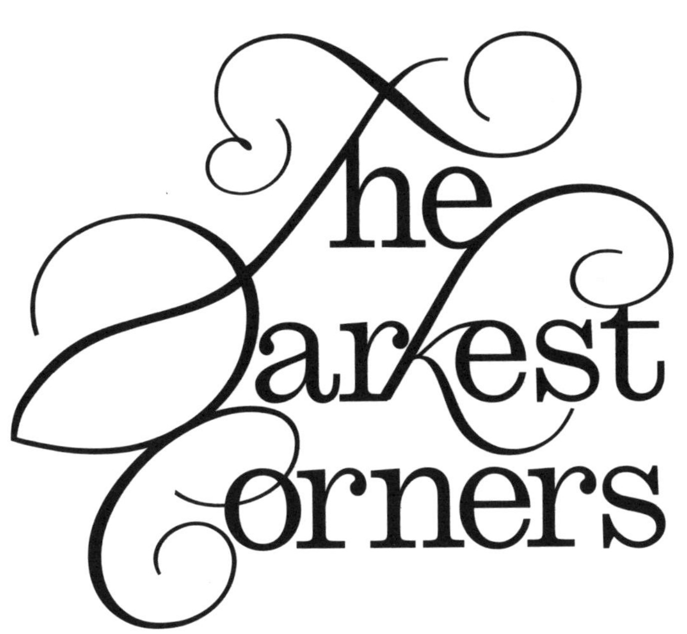

The Darkest Corners

To the city of Venice

Published on the occasion of
Lena Marie Emrich: The Darkest Corners

October 6–November 4, 2023

Curated by Marlene A. Schenk

At the following locations:
aarduork, Fondazione Giancarlo Ligabue, and in public spaces in Venice

Table of Contents

The Darkest Corners is a publication closely linked to a series of artworks by sculptor Lena Marie Emrich. It came into being by meandering through the maze that is the city of Venice, focusing on the architecture the lagoon presents to the curious eye. It was heavily inspired by these diverse elements, and the potential for losing one's way.

Drifting through Venice, we found little protrusions and bumps spread throughout the city in the corners of narrow alleyways and near churches. Known as *pissabraga*, *pissotte*, or *gobbe antibandito*, these multifunctional and uniquely Venetian "bulges" dot the city's least visible niches. They are the focus of Emrich's sculptures, which are located in exhibition venues as well as public space. But it is also Venice's streets, its spirit, and its architecture that are the focus of the artworks. Of particular importance are Venetian architect Carlo Scarpa and *architettura organica*, the architectural approach that deals with the historical substance of buildings, interpreting the possibilities of additively joining the new to the old.

The Darkest Corners, as both an exhibition format and as a series of artworks, uses the city's nooks and crannies to weave the sculptural into Venice, shining a light on an invisible yet always present part of the city. Emrich's work reinterprets the invisible presence of the *gobbe* so as to heighten their structural importance to Venice and highlight on an overlooked part of the city. Within this intervention, the essential meaning of the object is revealed as one of the city's integral "glues."

So, too, are the *tiranti*, the architectural motifs of the façades of Venetian buildings, which Mario Ciaramitaro and Alberto Restucci discuss in "Wondering Venice, Holding Its Façade, through Seasons."

The dialogue that follows, "On Cohesion," combines multilayered thoughts on existing in Venice, but also on collaborating on an exhibition as a curator and artist. It is an archive, where colliding perspectives intersect with basic information and personal impressions. Like a map, these thoughts create landmarks. They constitute a joint effort to place together many perspectives in order to find the parts, objects, and, significantly, stories that hold Venice together.

As *The Darkest Corners* became more than an exhibition, this book became something else, too, within both space and writing. *The Darkest Corners* works with raw materials, respecting craftsmanship, legacy, and production; it is contemporary in its use of history. There is always the research, the form, the creation, and the craft. But there is also unceasingly the self, the other, and the constant, tender desire to understand someone else; the desire for partnership, and imagination; the acknowledgment of being lost, and being okay with it, of being on a path to somewhere without clear direction.

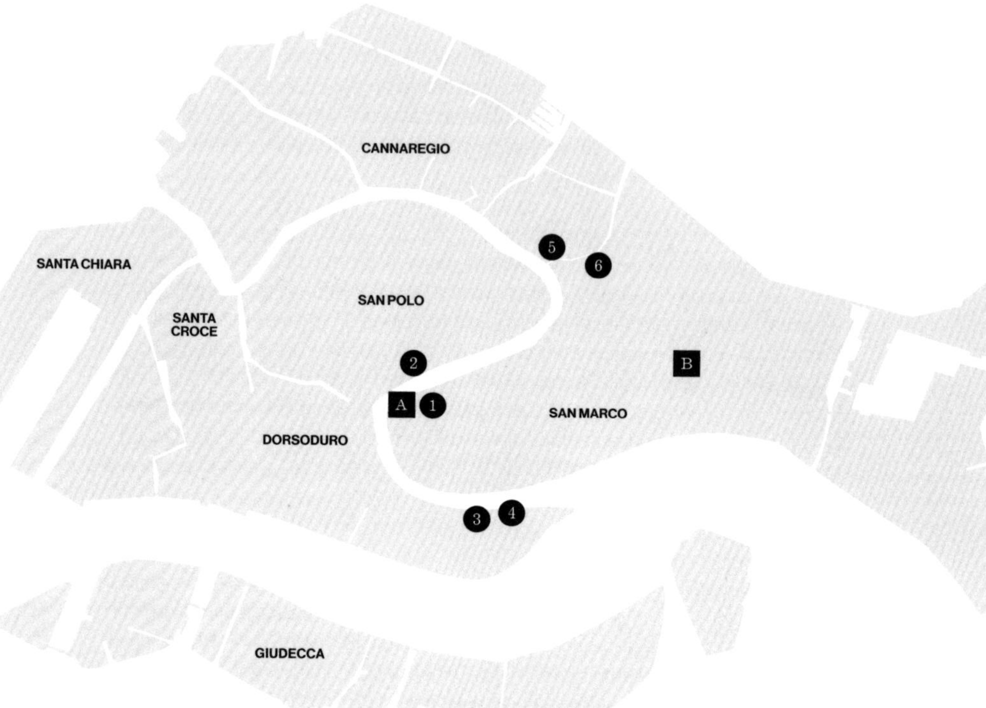

CANNAREGIO
SANTA CHIARA
SAN POLO
SANTA
CROCE
SAN MARCO
DORSODURO
GIUDECCA

INSPIRATION GOBBES

1 45.4343959, 12.3282199
Near Giancarlo Ligabue Foundation

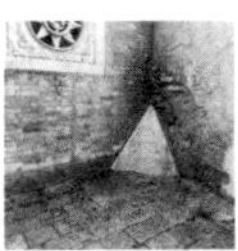

2 45.4361668, 12.3289005
Near Centro Tedesco

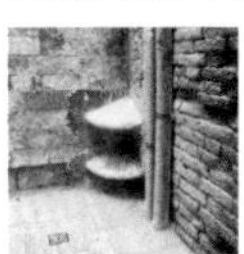

3 45.4307680, 12.3338960
Near Salute

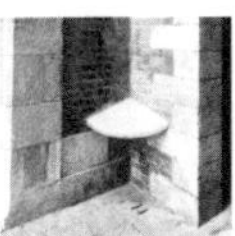

4 45.4305427, 12.3321986
Near Collezione Peggy Guggenheim

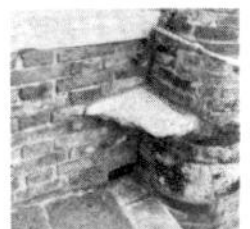

5 45.4397083, 12.3382322
Near Palazzo Bembo-Baldù

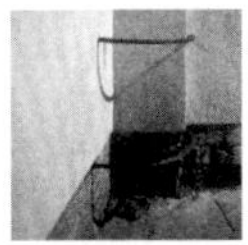

6 45.4403919, 12.3358655
Near Palazzo Michiel

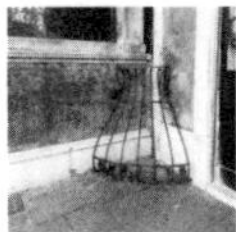

EXHIBITION SPACES

A Fondazione Giancarlo Ligabue
San Marco, 3319

B aarduork
Salizada Zorzi, 4931

The Darkest Corners

Marlene A. Schenk

For the most part, everything begins
with a search.

The hotel was being renovated. We had been
looking for it for a while, roaming the streets. Now
we were standing in front of a huge, white plastic
tarpaulin, meant to hide the structure from foreign
eyes, or so as not to spoil the outcome. Beside it,
resting next to ever-present dark canal waters in
the shadows by the pier, an adjacent gondolier
was looking around, waiting for guests who would
not be arriving for the time being. He leaned his
right foot against a humped, round stone. The
Palazzo has put a billboard around its silhouette
and over the white plastic tarp, which informs
passersby: Venice is built on 118 islands
connected by over 400 bridges.

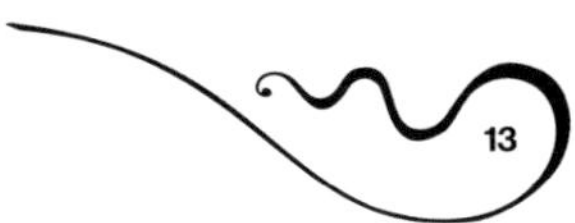

For this particular story, the dawn of a search begins in the dark.

The streets here are never-ending, though simultaneously ending too soon; the other side, divided by a stretch of shiny liquid mass, becomes unreachable. Corners become smaller, streets denser, lights flickering; there is sweat, darkness meeting light, fullness meeting emptiness. When you walk through Venice long enough, you get lost continually, reaching nowhere but the darkest corners of the city. There's an ever-present mix of fishy smells and of fresh laundry hanging from above, never giving way to the sunlight. A child from a windowsill spits into the turquoise canal that turns dark green when the wind blows the washed shirts, submerging everything into more shade. Fruit stands, wooden doors, cigar smoke: we have been here before.

Located in the dark alleyways, in the corners leading to the churches, are architectural leftovers, inconspicuous protrusions. They are wearing their own armor, casts of mortar, often made from white Istrian stone or wrought iron.

Everything I say from here on is speculative.

Venice has always been a place of legends—yes, going further, in the case of Venice, it is almost impossible to make a clean distinction between fact and fable. The darkest corner is a fact; the search for the element in question endless. Led by obsession,[1] we wanted to make the seemingly invisible element of the city space—the architectural element, the humps, the myth—visible. Primarily installed to prevent burglaries and murders at night and subsequently for hygienic reasons, the architectural elements known as *pissabraga*, *pissotte*, or *gobbe antibandito* are the key elements of this story. The unlit, darkest corners were a perfect hiding place from which to mug a passerby. Imagine: an island out of control. Venice didn't have full public lighting until the implementation of gas lights in 1839,[2] and it is said that, at night, the city became saturated with crime. Due to problems with fires,[3] furnaces and similar light-giving instruments had been mostly banned from the city prior to this. The *gobbe antibandito*[4] were built together with the appearance of other professions, for example the so-called *codega*,[5] a servant who lit the darkened streets with a lantern before families walked through them.

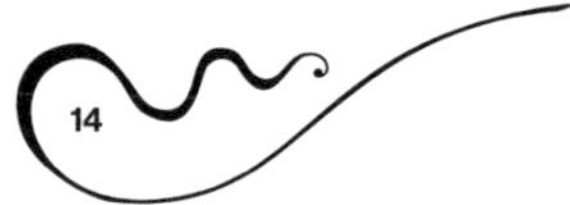

(1)

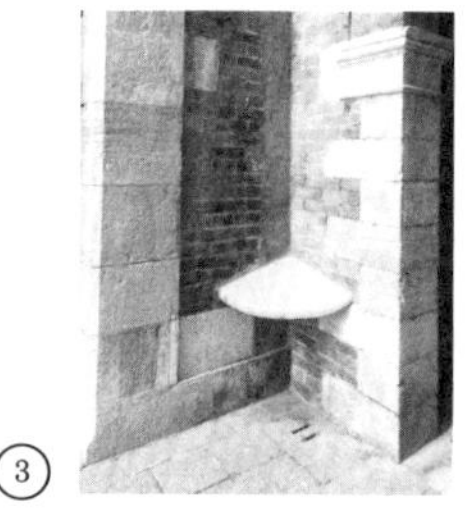

(3)

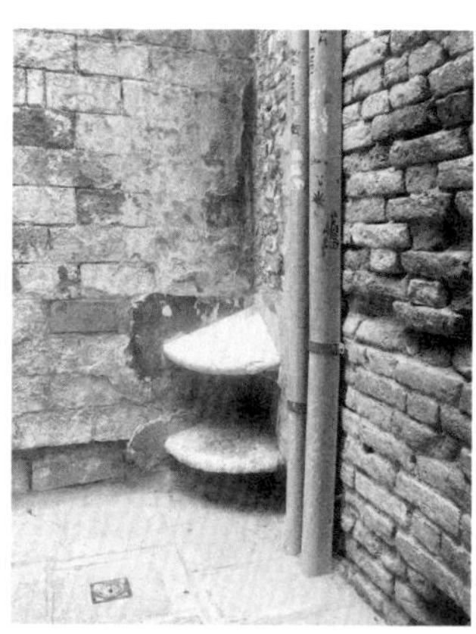

(2)

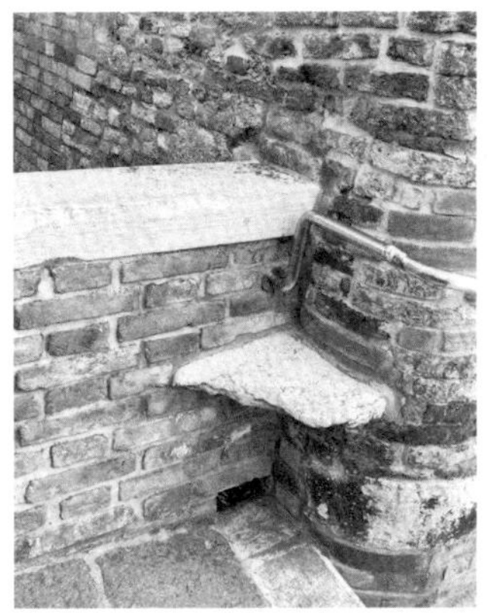

(4)

It was either in addition to preventing criminality—once the city was lit, criminals could be seen, caught, fought—that the *gobbe* also had the task of preventing Venetians from urinating in the corners of the streets, rendering it a multifunctional educational tool on how to treat one's city and, by proxy, the people living within it. The inscrutability of history's connections, the object's versatility, but at the same time its blunt one-sidedness, fascinated us. Surprisingly, few Venetians had a relationship with the *gobbe*; they seemed to be invisible to them.

The inner dynamics of Venice slow down, intensify, and fight every search.

I had been looking for facts and written records of the gobbe for months now. I was caught between what professors of architecture, Venetians, archivers, art historians, cartographers, files, libraries, tourist guides, the internet, and the city landscape itself told me. Everything seemed to take forever, yet time was slipping through my fingers. As a place of ever-evolving stasis, Venice has the most distinctive attribute of counting time as a different entity, allowing thinking and creating to mature differently. You must

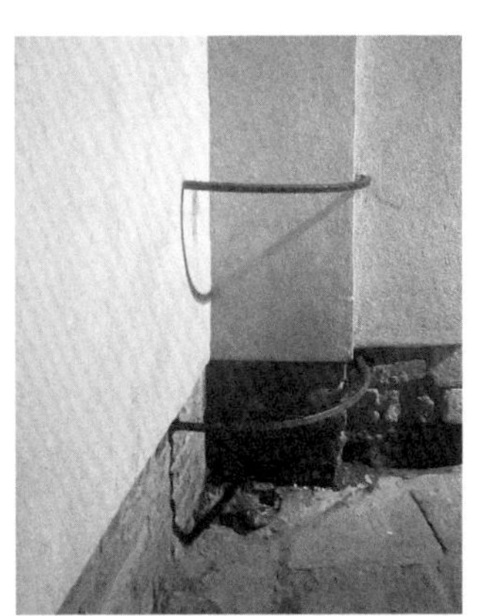

(5)

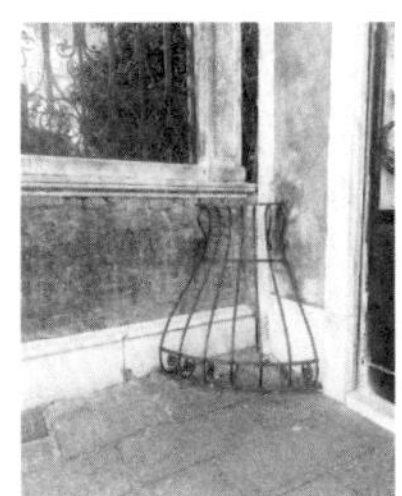

(6)

find your place in it: it is these contradictions that make Venice a place of paradigmatic amalgamations. Here, past, present, and future are celebrated for their poetic functions in a space touching the sea. It is the contradictions of Venice that makes the approach to an exhibition seemingly easy in its beauty, yet harder in its implementation.

I was lost in the sea of tales, not sure how to determine right from wrong. I was desperate, had not slept for days. My skin smelled of panicked sweat and the Archivio di Stato di Venezia, where I was dismayed to learn that not all Latin is the Latin I studied and where I had tried in vain to find any written information, papers, or laws on *gobbe*. Framing the city as chaotic and without order was not possible at this point, because somehow all ends still met here in inexplicable ways. I was lost; time was dissolving. Whenever I left the walls of the building, I encountered more walls.

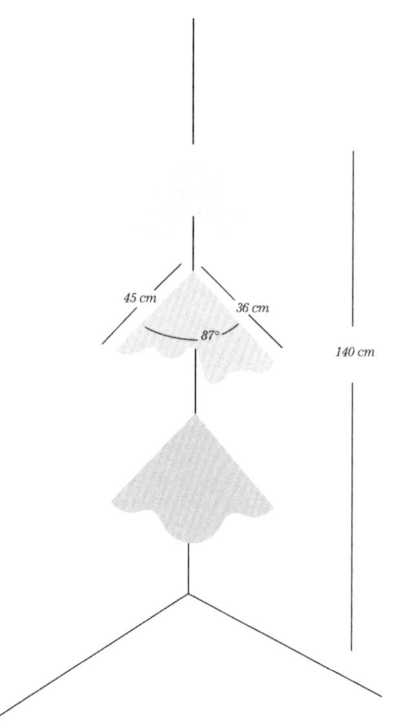

Turning corners four times somewhere between Formosa and Castello, the Libreria Editrice Filippi lies in an alley just a corner away from the more touristy streets. The owner, Franco Filippi, has never sat anywhere else, smoking endlessly among an ocean of books. It was his writing on the *gobbe* in the book *The Curiosities of Venice* that furnished me, as well as our friends Mario and Alberto, with any information about them.[6] During our brief talk, Filippi had already smoked three cigarettes. Talking about the *gobbe*, he shook his head repeatedly, gesticulating and declaring in short, exclamatory sentences. "There is no writing about them, except, perhaps, oral history, of the *gobbe*, or *pissotte*, or *pissabraga*. Whatever legends are called, that is all this is. Maybe it has something to do with the hygiene, *probably* with criminality, but, in the end, these are all myths from the mainland. *It could be* that there is something

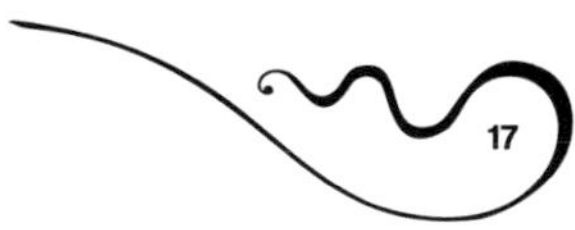

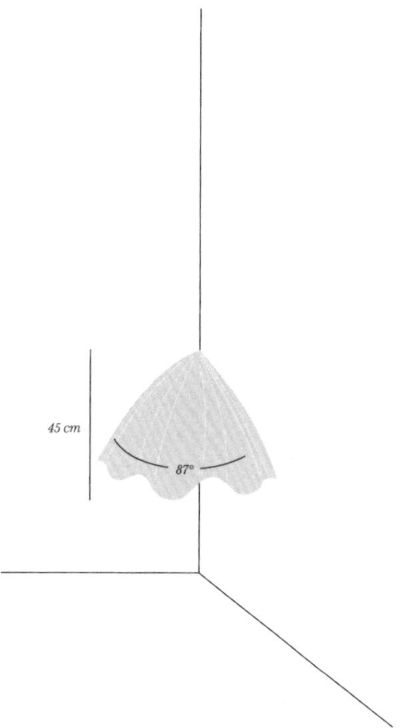

in written form—*perhaps* it could have been in the Archivio di Stato." It was during his third cigarette that I surrendered.

While I climbed the third ladder of the fourth library Venice has to offer, Lena turned her thoughts to the genesis of the *gobbe*, attempting to turn this strange element into something extraordinary. For her, it was not important to prove the existence of something that is already there.
Seeing it, touching it, had been enough; she had made a pact with the city.

As time dissolves, it is the path, and no longer the search, that suddenly becomes important.
Lena had started to create an archive of all the *gobbe* we could find. They were hiding everywhere, unseen, structural elements so vastly different from one another, yet exhibiting a serene unity. Crescents, waves, triangles, trapezoids, multiple trapezoids: they all had their place. Photos documenting our hour-long walks showed signs of professionalism: we had made it our job to find what was invisible to most.

There were a few things we were sure of.
Firstly, that, with regard to the works, we would place importance on the relationship between water and land, water and light within the lagoon. Choosing glass and working with local artisans and companies illustrated this specific entanglement, as glass is an indispensable material for Venice and yet the only material to imitate these three elements. In relation to some steel-woven *gobbe*, there would also be a hot-dip galvanized-steel sculpture corresponding to the other works. Installed in the right places, glass and metal should ensure the ever-present balancing act within the lagoon that redefines not only the

landscape, but the lives of Venetians.

Secondly, that we would need to alienate the object while keeping its general form, purpose, and affiliations in order to draw attention to it and in order for it to guide one through a dark corner. Fungi, scallops, shells: these organic forms add to the topography, primitive at first but almost resembling an outgrowth from walls. Despite being functional, they are precise in their surface structures, although all of them are abstractions of natural forms. Whirlpools swirling under water, wavy streams.

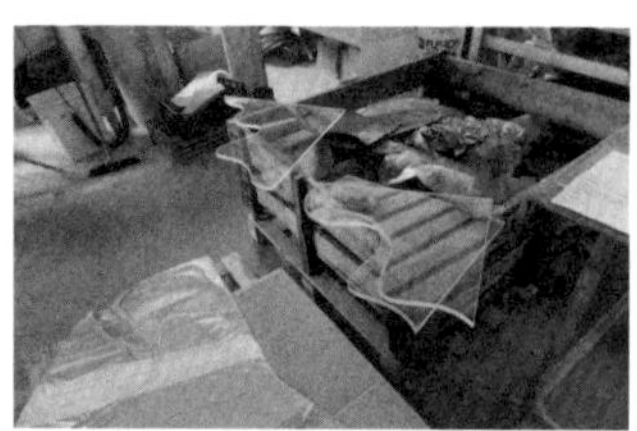

Thirdly, that the works should be planned out to be a poetic gesture toward the unknown, one that holds appreciation, sustainability, and responsibility for Venice within them.

We had decided on materials quickly, but choosing colors for a place that has been depicted as the site for unique light and shades throughout history proved more challenging. While selecting them, we often sat in silence. We thought of ever-present hues in Venice, tints distorted by time. The aim was to draw attention to the darkest corners without being too distracting: a natural color spectrum, sand and brick walls, the amber, blueish-green colors of the canals and lagoon. The mystification of the object seemed endless. It was then that the project began.[7]

There is no such thing as a path that leads nowhere.

The *pissabraga, pissotte,* or *gobbe antibandito* are not sculptures dedicated to rulers or deities. They were not invented by one of Venice's geniuses, such as Titian or Vasari; they are no glorification of the city. You might find one in the dark side street leading off from the solemn Doge's Palace, or next to the tavern where an aperitivo costs only 2.50 euros for Venetians but 8.50 euros for visitors. The *gobbe* are an integral part

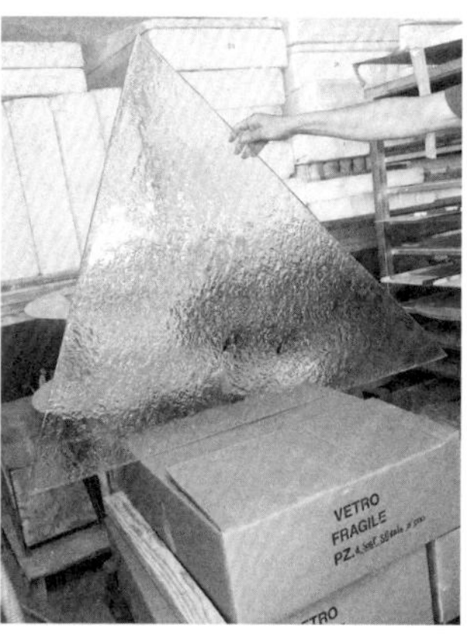

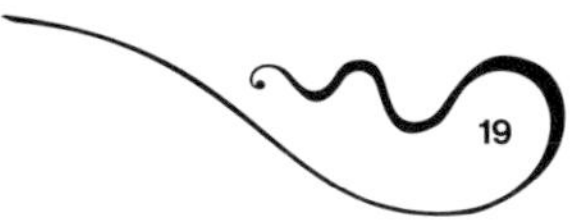

of Venice's cityscape. They were created within a place's particular context, out of a necessity they were made to fit into: to fight violence, to preserve hygiene. They have grown with the city and have expanded it, protected it, held it together.

At their core, the *pissing corners of Venice* represent the fusions that make up Venice: time and space, one-sidedness and versatility, defense and inclusion, positive resistance. Their inconspicuous placement and unimpressive exterior carry what holds the city together at its core.

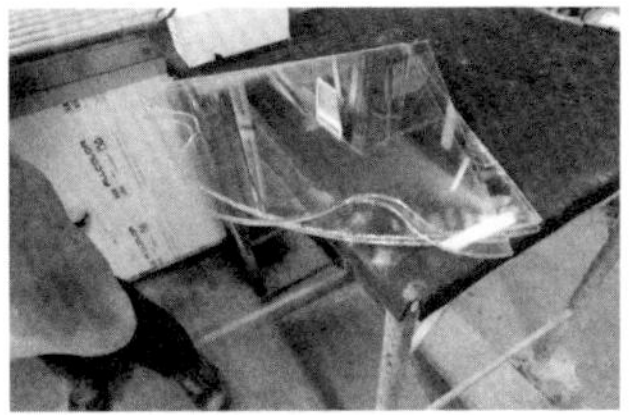

The sculptures are placed in various spaces within the city. In the Venetian Carlo Scarpa's[8] manner, but also looking at the spatial and temporal implications Venice imposes upon a person, the exhibition respects traditional craft, legacy, and production while maintaining a contemporary angle. Elevating the once rigid and seemingly forgotten everyday objects, they are made from

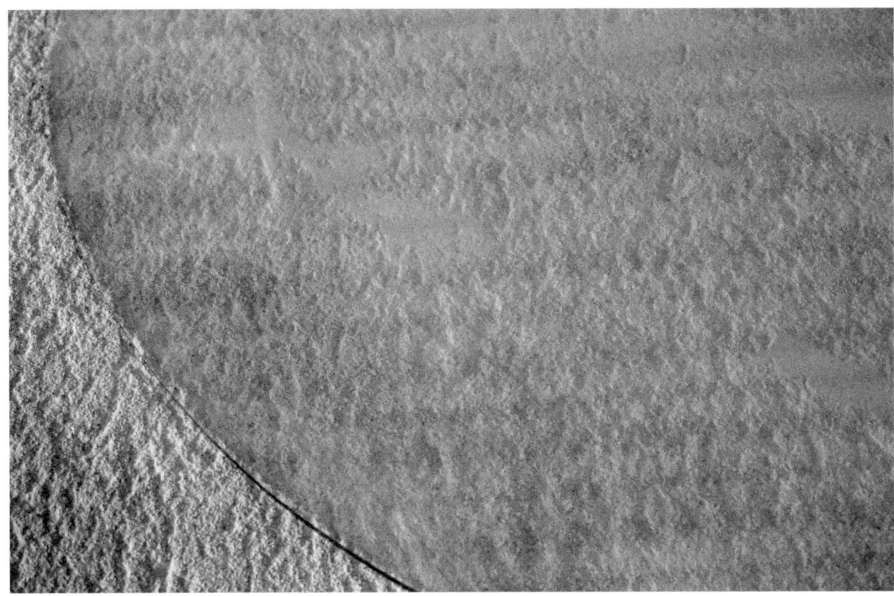

glass as a main element, combined with wood and steel. In the corners of the exhibition space, in the corners of the streets on the way to sheltered gardens, they come from hiding and are made visible. Just as there is not *the* place or *the* channel, nor a simple center in Venice, the sculptures are scattered through the whole of the island.

Walking the streets, the darkest corners are illuminated through the coloring of the glass and through the reflection of light. The sculptures become a part of the street and we become aware of their presence; the city allows for them to take their space. The sculptural shells become soft when one glances at their tender colors, the cravings in movement: combining what is seemingly contradictory and secondary is the quintessential trait of Lena Marie Emrich's practice. That can be the attention to detail in reserved holding structures, which take on the utmost urgency,

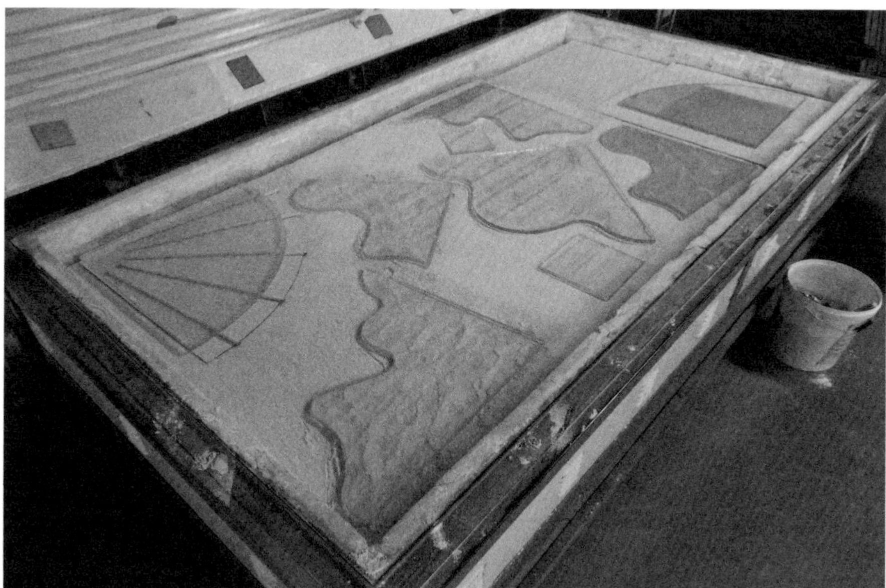

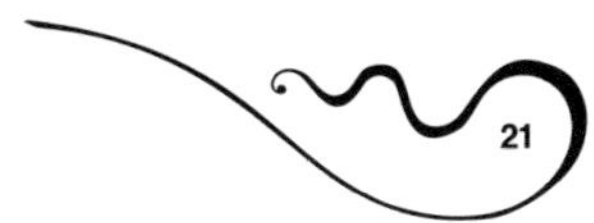

or the seemingly unbothered alignment with the most uneven wall that has been carefully thought through. It is along these lines of her manifestations that the act of really looking at our surroundings changes, and so does the meaning of the streets that were dark before. In her sculptural poetics and with the utmost care toward what is surrounding her at all times, she heightens the existence of the passive though evident object. Within this activation of an everyday object, Lena not only connected with the gobbe itself; she also attained a gentle spatial and human exchange: How much space do we give to others and how do we take care of this space? In The Darkest Corners, her works become the valve for a sensitive merging of the architectural, historical, as well as the imaginative within the one environment that is continually longing for poetry and magic: Venice.

Her work has been heavily influenced by the urban historical venue, its materials and landscape. Thoughtful combinations of materials develop a significant formal reasoning within the objects.

Spatial arrangements, as well as construction and mounting, demand a thought-out technique that respects the oldest walls, as well as each screw.

As objects, they carry within them a lightness and fragility, while also being integral and functional. Their meaning changes depending on the viewing angle and light: sometimes reflecting, sometimes appearing waterlike. In a way, the organic forms of the sculptures create a mimicry effect, with each sculpture reacting individually to the corner it is inhabiting. Like organisms, they grow out from the walls, just as the shells are growing in the lagoon. Venice is always a web of symbolic allusions, and the sculptures are artworks reflecting its endless connections,

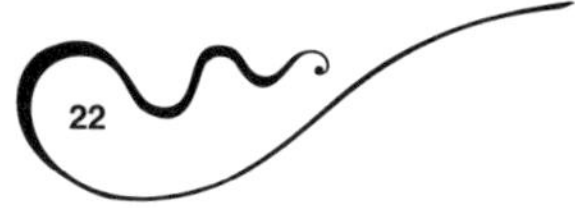

representing tradition in contemporary times
and reviving the unique energy of a city that carries hundreds of years of history within its streets,
whether it's documented for our contemporary
needs or not. In the darkest corners, the gobbe
protect the city and secure its functioning. They
are invisible yet powerful guardians. In highlight-
ing their existence, the artworks address a trav-
eler's consciousness, a respect toward the city's
salty walls.

As far as my knowledge of the *gobbe* goes, perhaps research into them were to follow the history
of the glassblowers. For fire safety reasons, all
the glass furnaces of Venice were moved to the
island of Murano in 1295. They had to leave the
island behind to hold onto it. With this in mind,
I left the archives, and with it the expectations,
the proof I thought everyone needed for the small,
bulging objects in the streets to *really* exist
somewhere, an outgrowth of an artist's imagination and an artisan's work, written on old parch-
ment paper.

I met Lena at Campo dei Frari. Lost in thought,
but not in the city, she had scribbled down various
forms of possible corner-installations and shell
forms. We strolled along the Piazza San Marco,
trying to ignore the masses. As we passed the
hotel—of course it was still under construction—
it dawned on me why I had needed the proof, why
it was necessary for the sculptural shell forms
to come. *Venice is built on 118 islands connected
by over 400 bridges.* There are countless docu-
ments on its creation, recreation, restauration.
Venice holds countless *pissabraga*, *pissotte*, or
gobbe antibandito. The builders of these objects,
these parts of the city, remain anonymous to this
day. For now, they are still hiding in the *darkest
corners*, fragments of their time—but I think we
are carefully bringing them to the light.

Notes

1   Pursuing knowledge, artistic vision, pressure of contemporary artistic research, etc.

2   Fiona MacAulay, Francesco Gerali, Jonathan Craig, Rasoul B. Sorkhabi, eds., *History of the European Oil and Gas Industry* (London: Geological Society, 2018), 158.

3   The Doge's Palace in 1483, the Scuola Grande di San Marco in 1485, the Fondaco dei Tedeschi in 1505, and the Rialto area in 1514. See Howard Burns, "Architecture," in *The Genius of Venice 1500–1600*, ed. Jane Martineau and Charles Hope (London: Royal Academy of Arts London, in association with Weidenfeld and Nicolson, 1980).

4   A definitive account of the *gobbe* will be researched. The State Archive has looked into its files to determine the first installations ordered by the city but has not yet found any clues. Neither have I. The forwarded research said (translated from Italian): "We would like to inform you that the search conducted in the available indexes and accompanying tools has yielded negative results regarding the architectural structures called 'gobbe-antibandito' or 'pissotte.' Below are sources where you can continue your research for the period of the Republic of Venice. For source descriptions, you may refer to the pages of the Information System of the State Archives of Venice (*moreveneto*) and to the relevant links to the accompanying resources. Provveditori di Comun (1272–1797), Signori di notteal criminal (1270–1797), Provveditories sopraprovveditori alla sanità (1486–1798), Provveditori, Sopraprovvveditori e Collegio alle pompe (1562–1797), Giudici del piovego (1514–1797) and Arti, Mureri, bb. 406–12, as well as the book Giovanni Caniato, Michela Dal Borgo (ca cura *Le arti edili a Venezia con saggi di Giorgio Gianighian, Giuseppe Sebesta e del Circolo culturale Menocchio presentazione Paolo Maretto*, Roma, Edilstampa, 1990)."

5   A term still in use today as a Venetian expression is "far el còdega," to be a third wheel.

6   Marina Crivellari Bizio, Franco Filippi, and Andrea Perego, eds., *Curiosità veneziane* (Venice: Filippi Editore, 1970).

7   Voice message from Lena: "For months I've been preparing the forms that will be made from glass now. I started in Austria to make the first drawings, cutting them out on cardboard, drawing them in angles, putting them in corners to identify clearly what should happen with them. Now, together with the glass blowers, we decided on two pieces of glass melting together on a structure of form sand. In the workshop, we are working on two levels. It is mid-July, and the heat is supported by the heavy machines downstairs and the ovens upstairs. Soon we cut out everything and will start blowing the pieces. There has been sweat in the air; the form sand mixed with our sweat. The itchy satisfaction of physical labor makes my skin crawl. It is a fine line to know your place in a glass workshop, when to intervene at the right time, and to know how to let go, as well as when to be the voyeur. With artisans, you don't need to speak the same language. We understand each other with the needs of the project, and this is where it starts."

8   "Carlo Scarpa's rearrangement of the ground floor and garden of the sixteenth-century Palazzo Querini Stampalia is a lesson in contemporary intervention, demonstrating the architect's supreme ability to weave the new into the old." Carlo Scarpa, *Querini Stampalia Foundation*, ed. Richard Murphy and Giorgio Busetto (London: Phaidon, 1993).

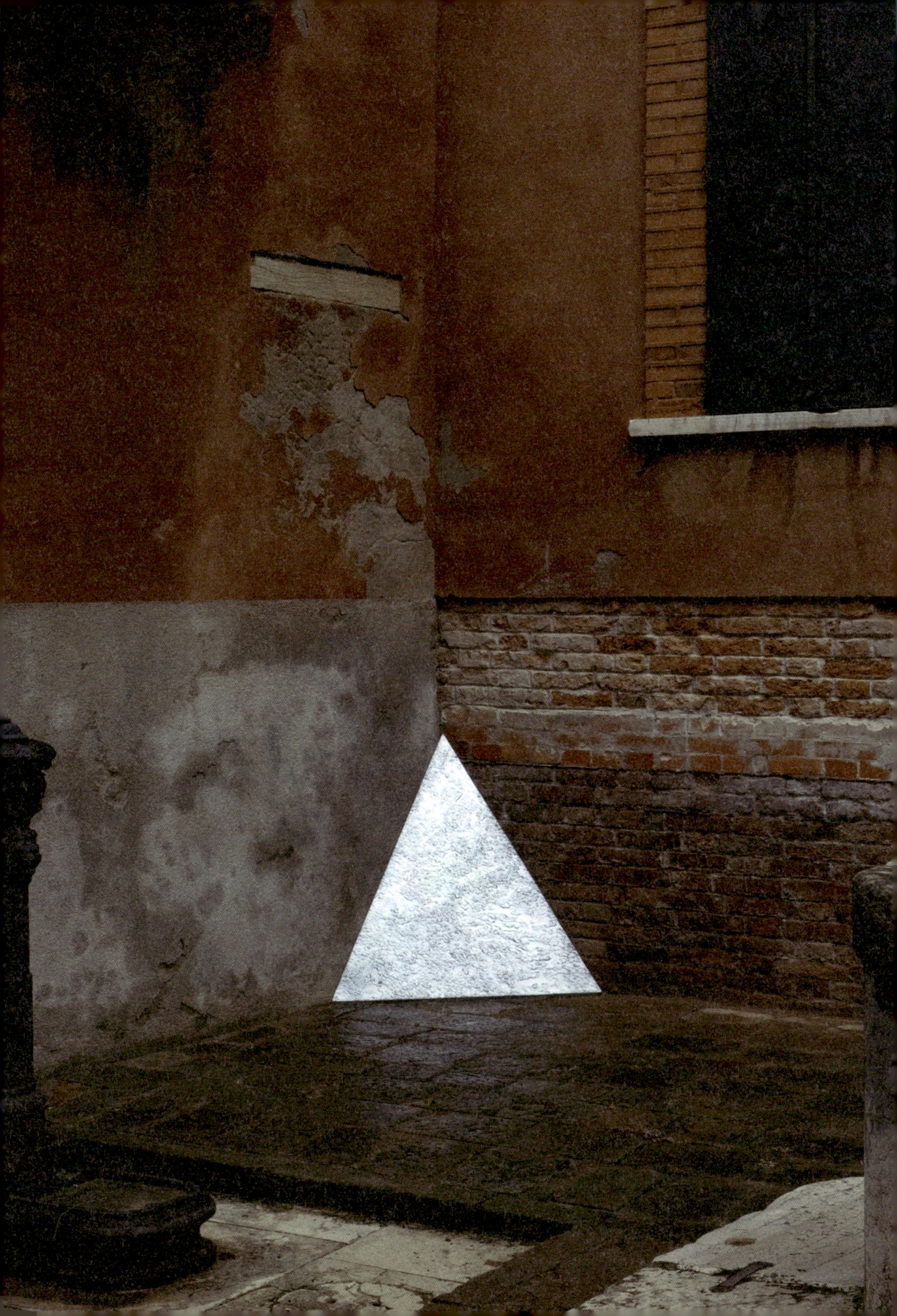

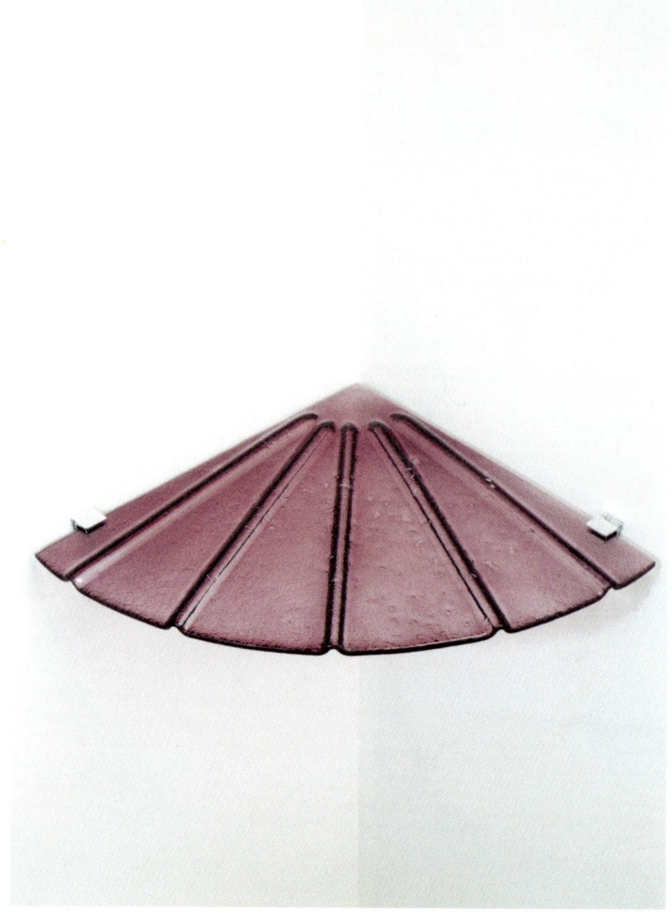

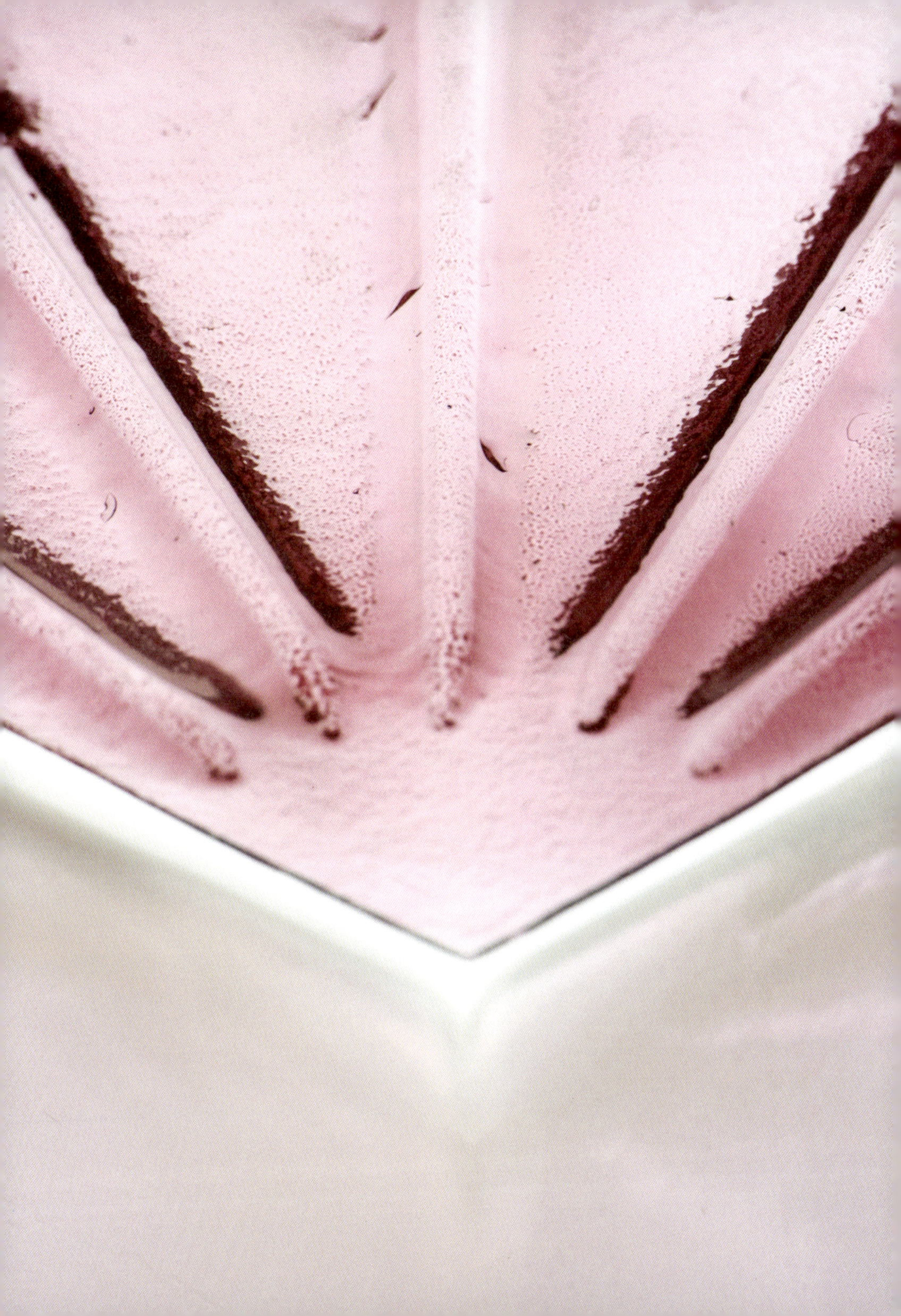

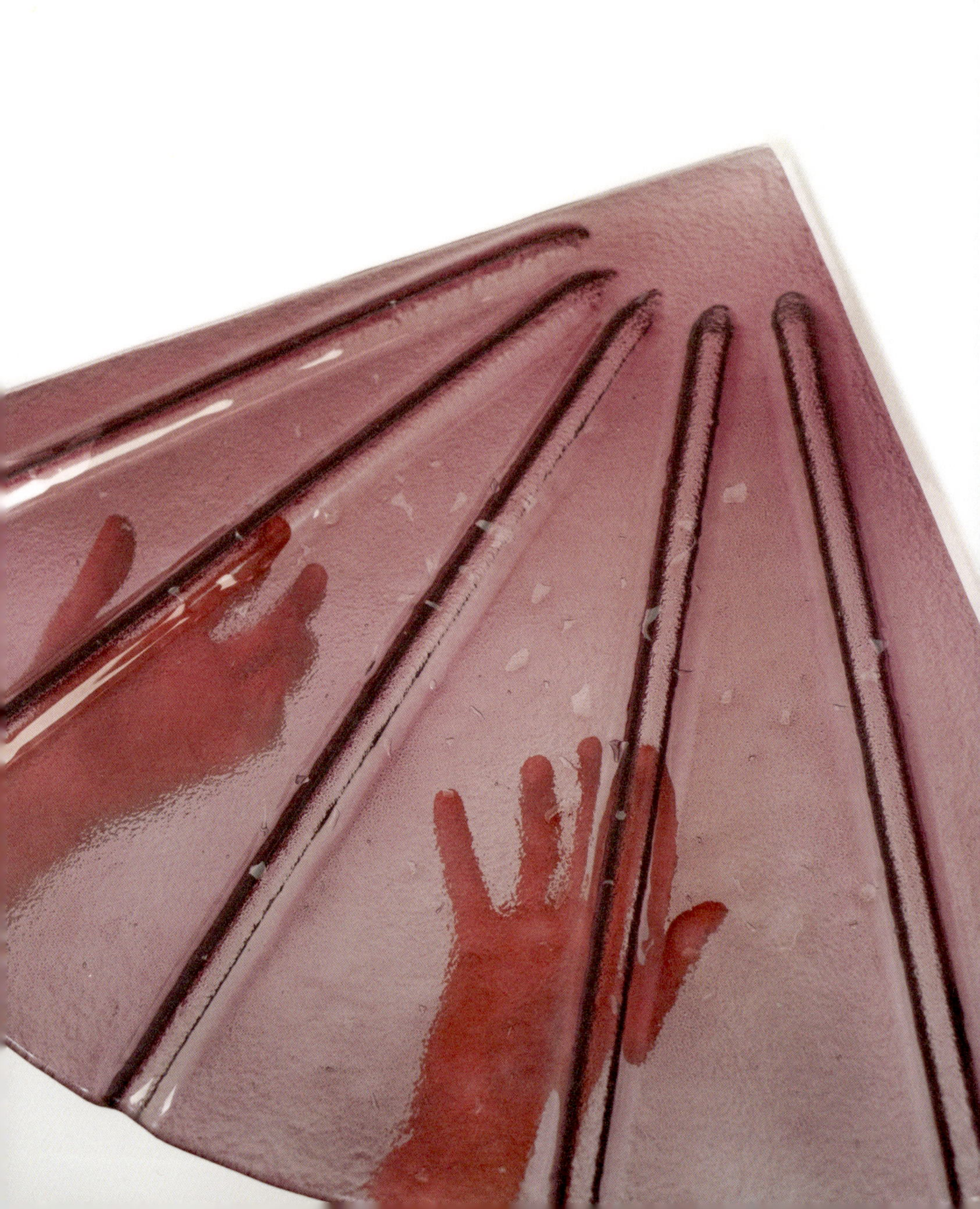

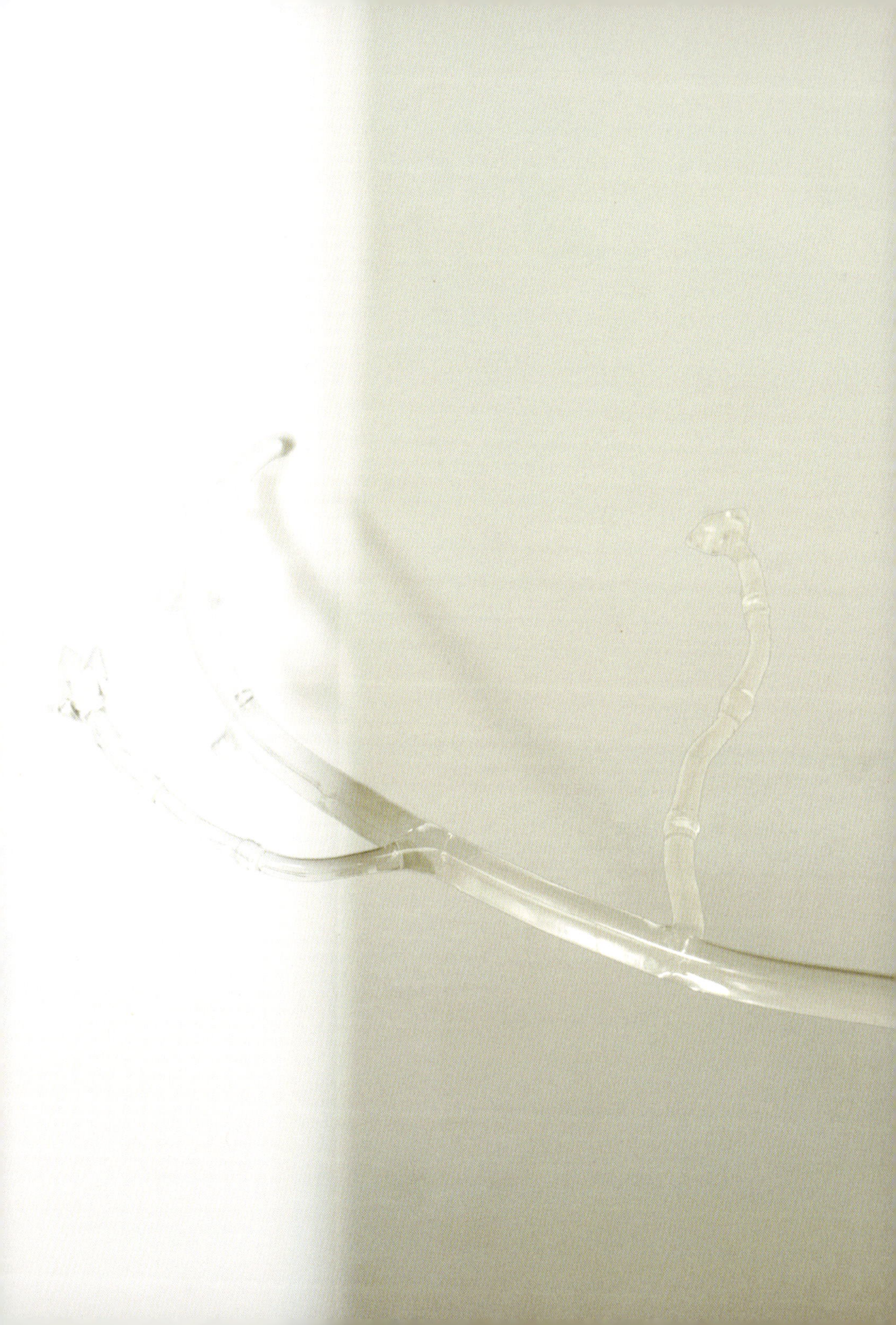

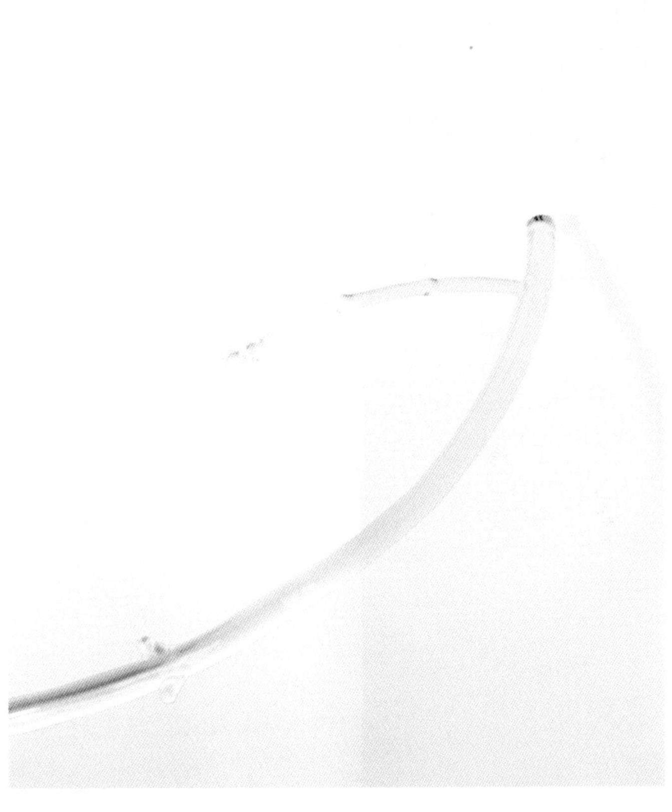

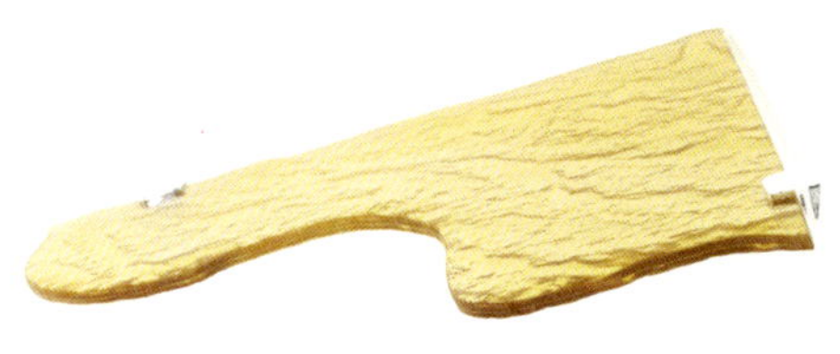

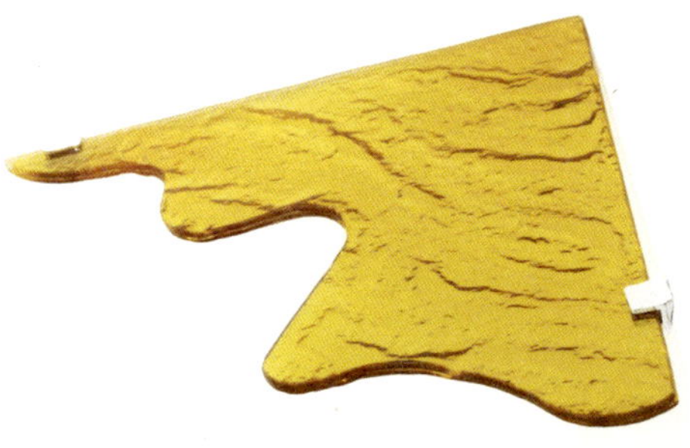

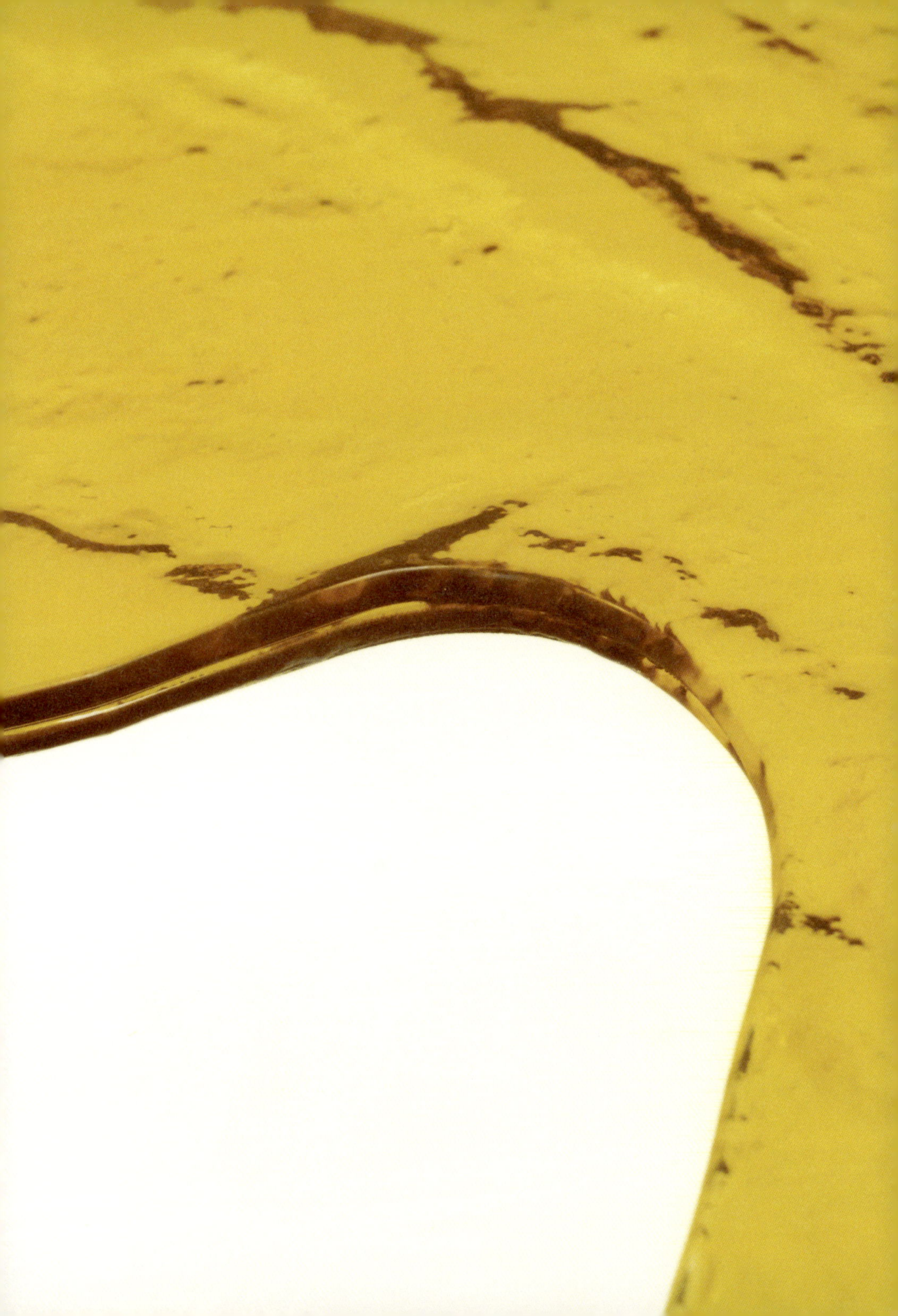

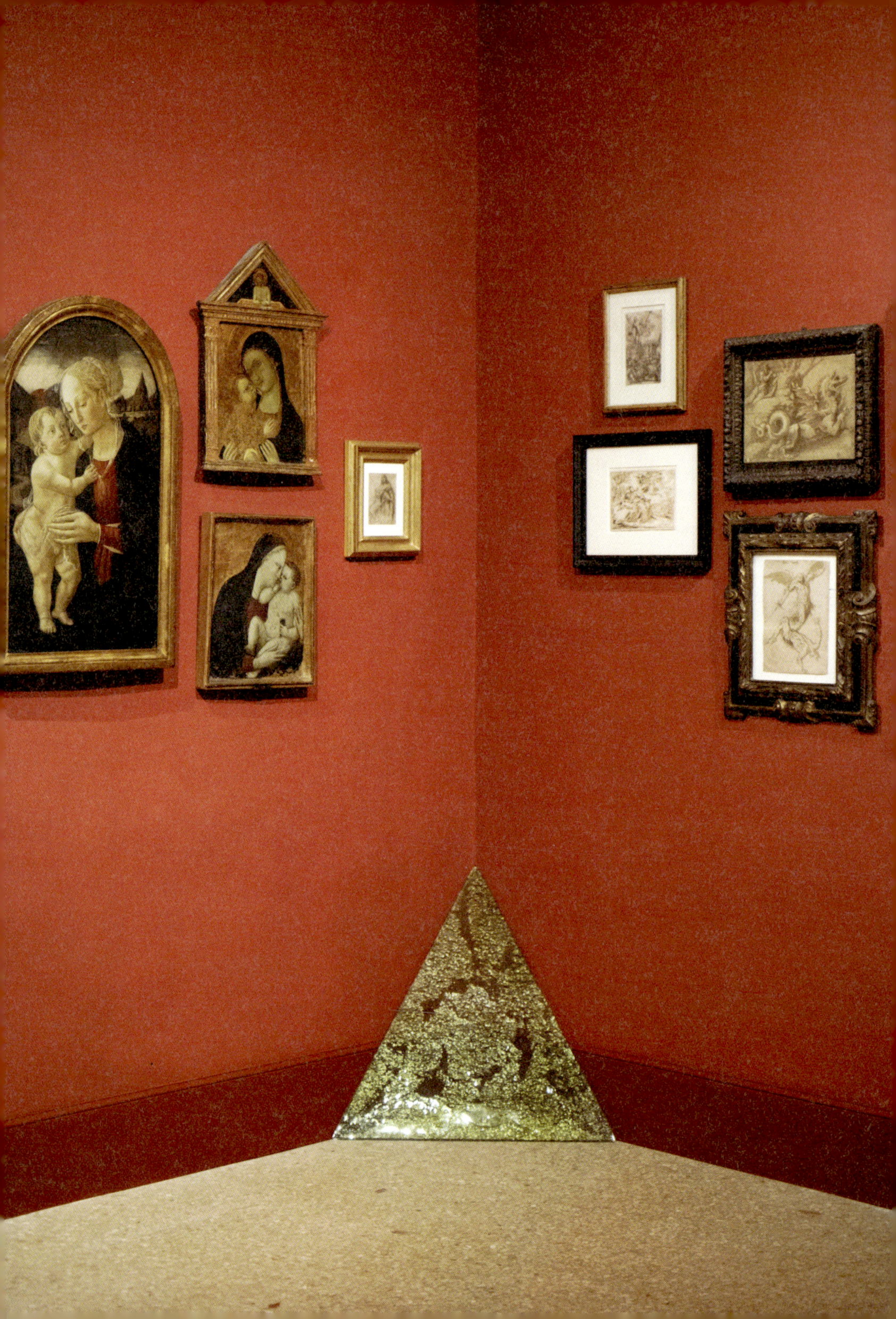

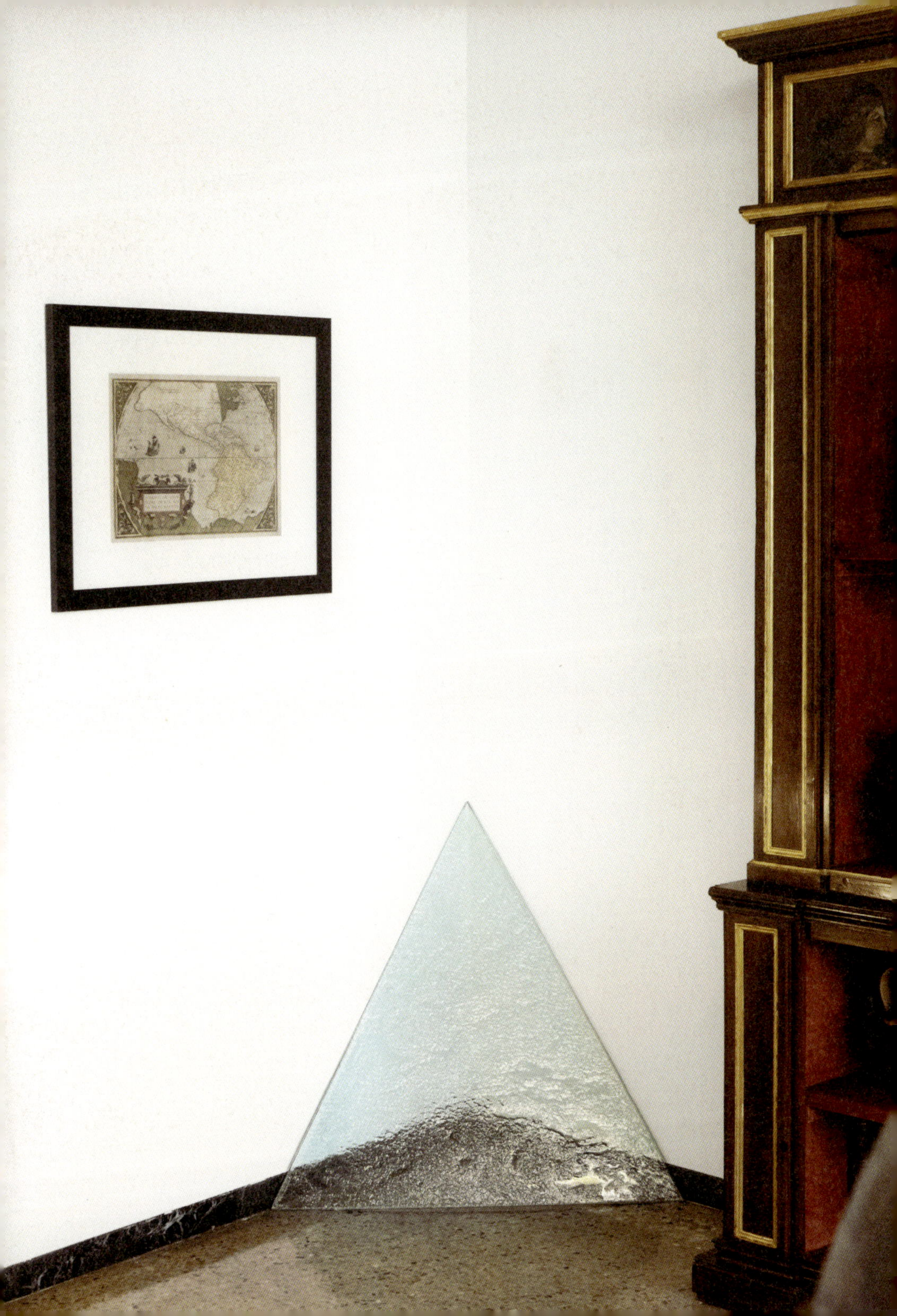

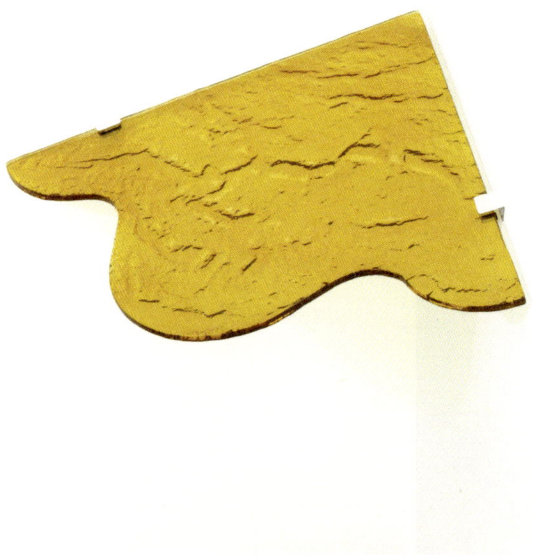

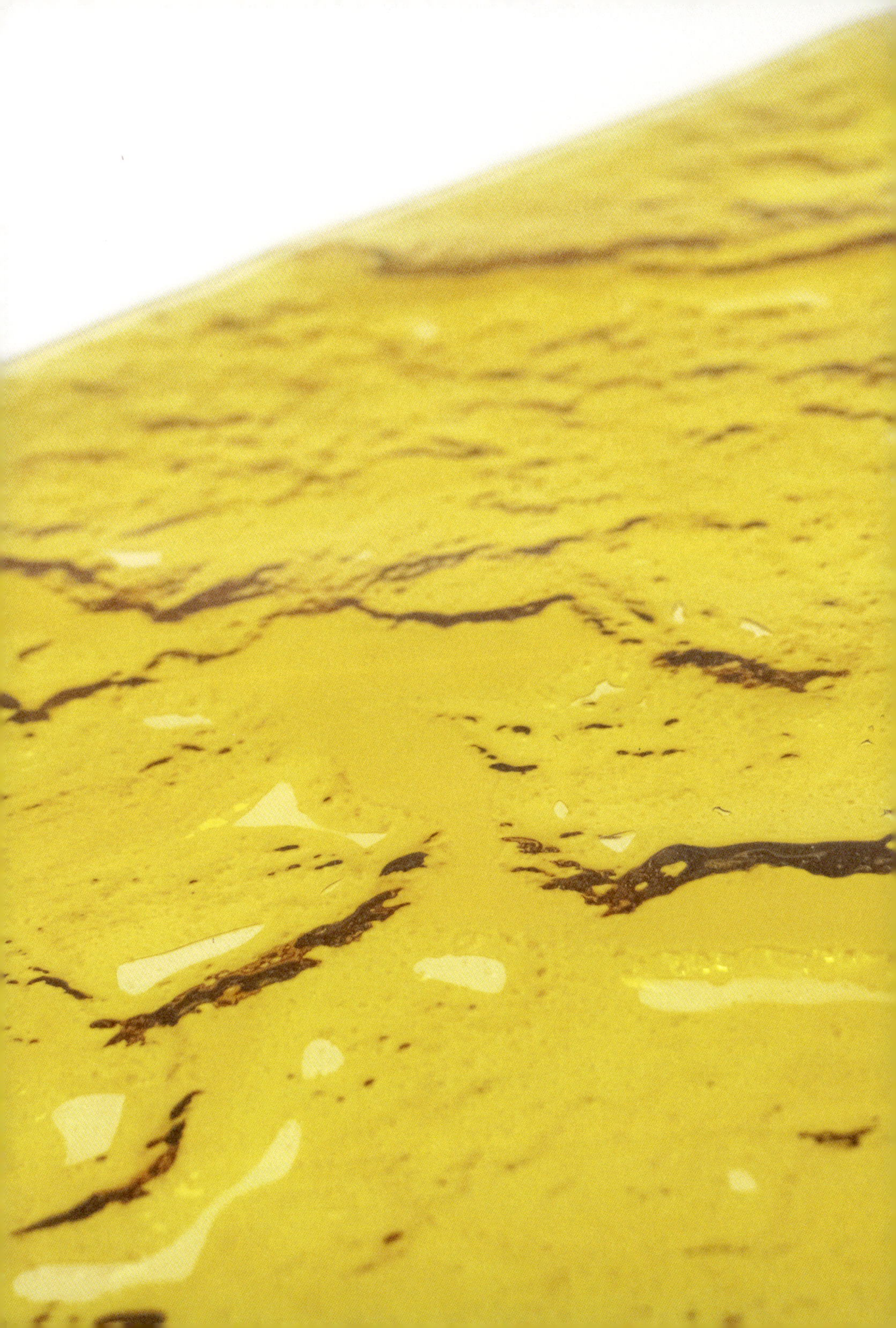

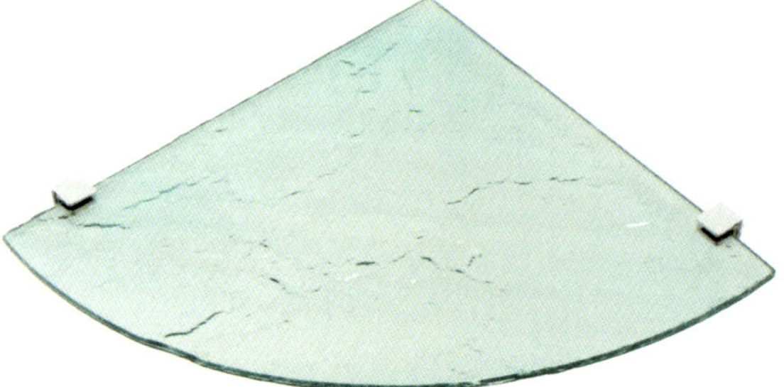

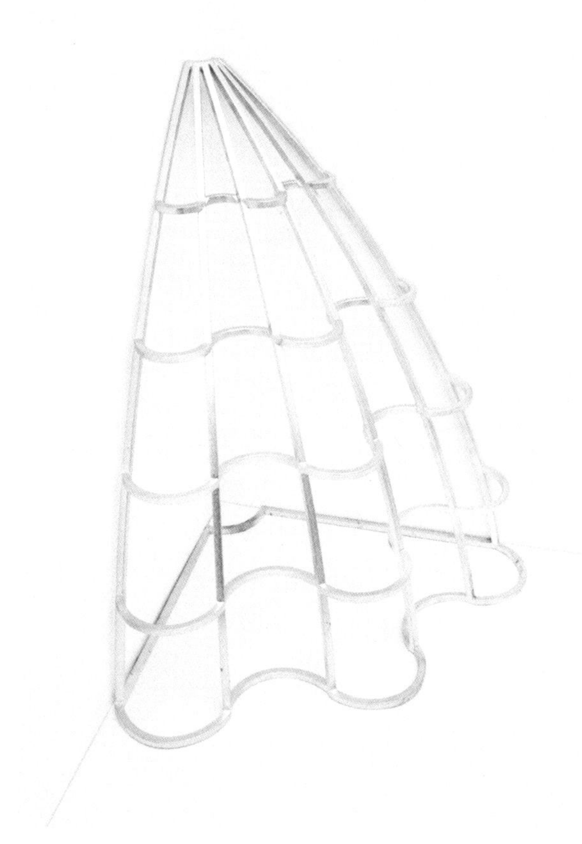

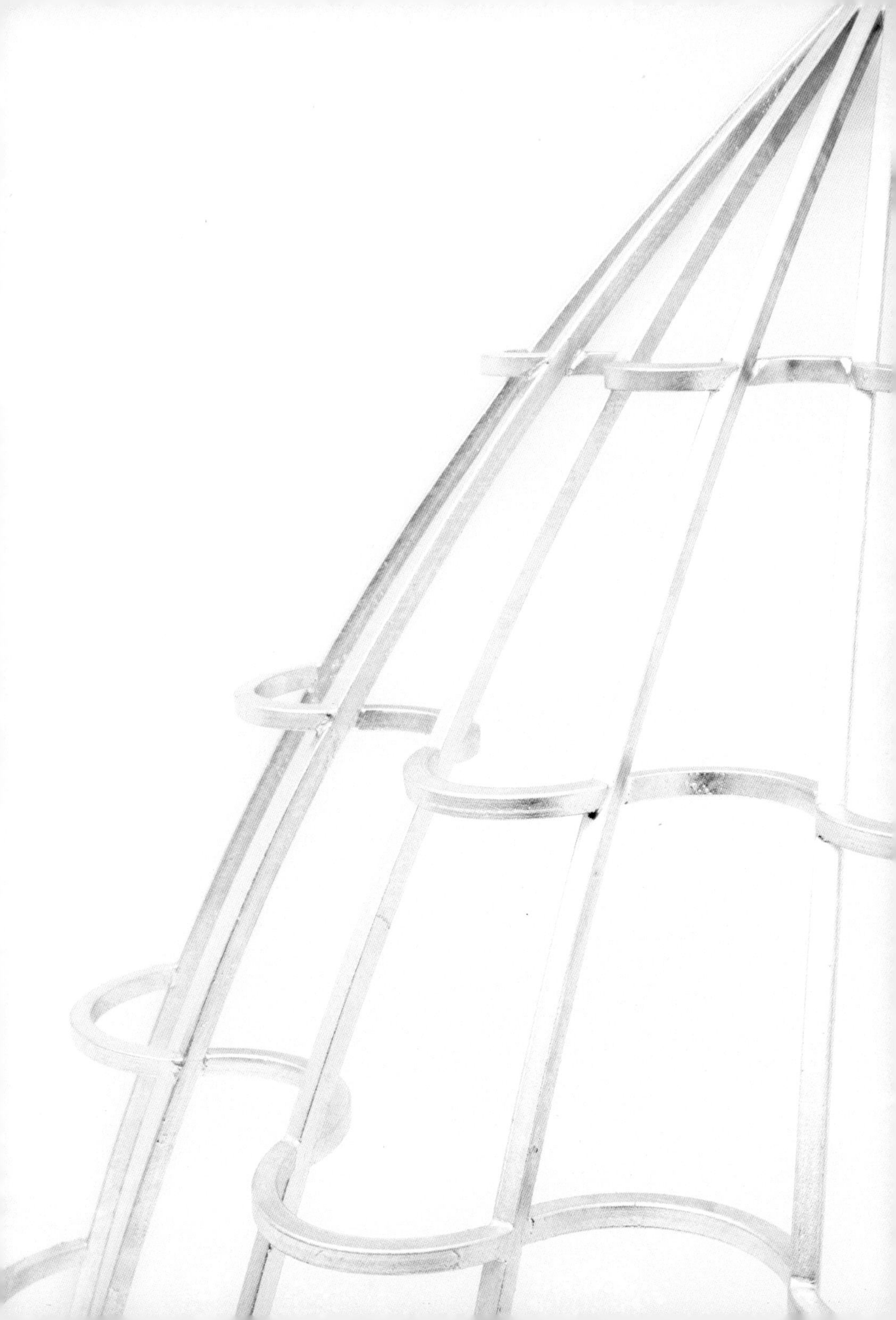

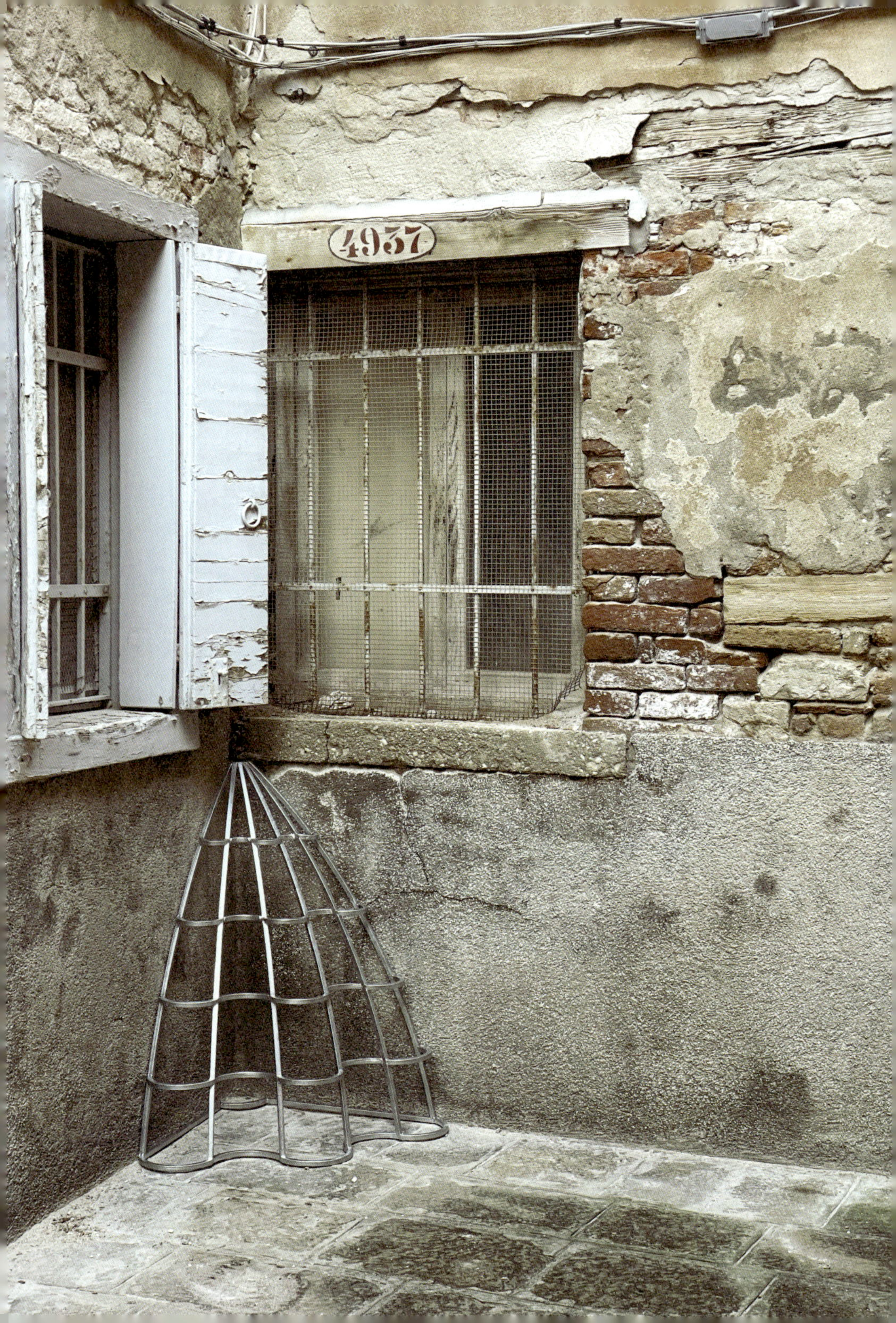

4937

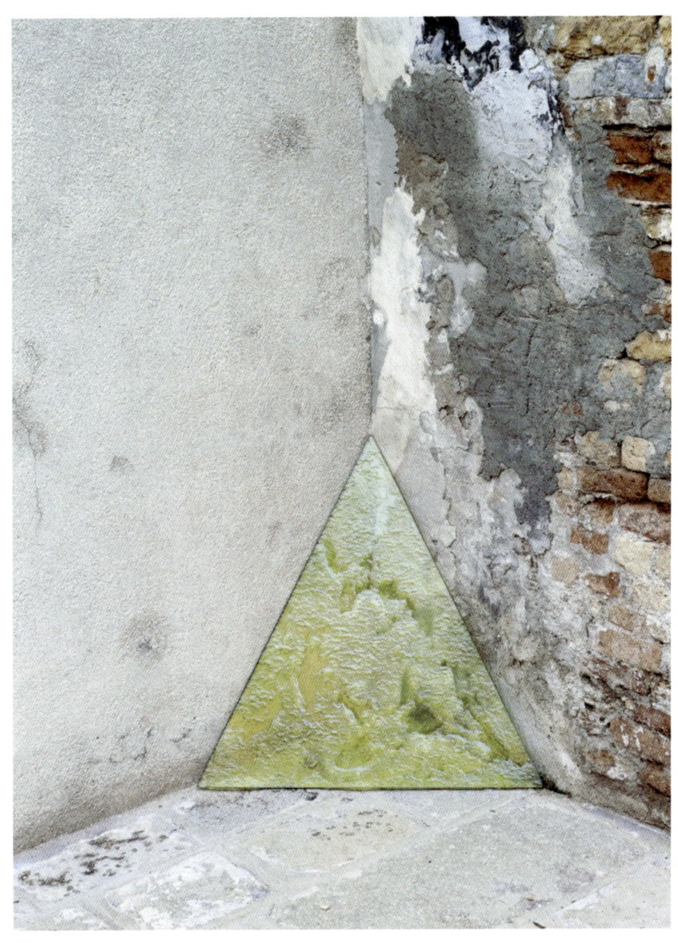

Wondering Venice, Holding Its Façade, through Seasons

Mario Ciaramitaro and Alberto Restucci

To host Lena Marie Emrich and her work at aarduork means embracing a profound practice in deciphering the city where our independent space has its roots. Moreover, it entails fostering an open and generous exchange with artists and authors. Experiencing the city through all its seasons is the only way to truly appreciate its layered and astonishing nature. This choice opposes mere sightseeing or a swift traversal of the urban fabric, which both deny the opportunity to embrace what the city freely offers to all: the time for contemplation of its forms and the allure of its stratifications.

Emrich's acute sensitivity to the spontaneous sculptural bodies scattered throughout the city becomes apparent when one navigates its labyrinthine alleys on a misty winter night face-to-face with a *pissotta*. These intriguing elements of micro-architecture, almost akin to functional sculptures, hearken back to a bygone era when urban solutions were crafted in a precarious and arbitrary manner, reflecting a long history of haphazard stratifications rooted in the popular and neighborhood milieu, independent of ordinances or formal architectural designs. Those small spontaneous interventions were closing the dark corners, countering the implosion of Venice at the hands of rampant nighttime crime. It was a very different city back then, so much so that Rio Terrà degli Assassini takes its name from the large number of killings or from particular professions like the *codega*.[1]

Dealing with darkness, as you know, is a social challenge, and even today, it is tackled with an infinite number of prohibitions and administrative orders,[2] even if today Venice has changed its rhythm and the night is the only moment when a resident can deeply connect with the city. The once dark corners, now illuminated, are no longer a problem, but they continue to be

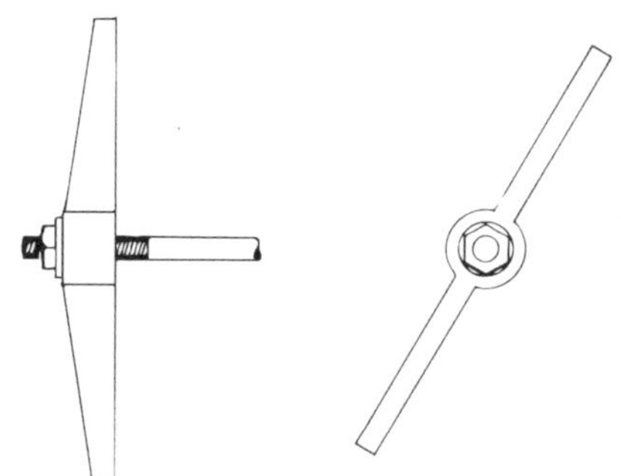

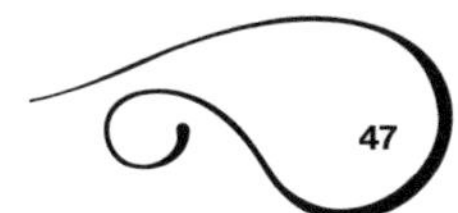

covered with *pissotte* that occasionally collide, in daytime, with those hurrying to work, those pushing carts of goods destined for the shops, those engrossed in the vigorous running, strenuous climbs, and fierce marathons that this "city of rest" imposes.[3]

Aarduork, our small, two-room gallery, is placed in one of the busiest *calli* that connect San Marco with the Ponte dei Greci, Campo della Bragora, and finally with the Arsenale. It witnesses both the perpetual visitor flow and the buildings' inherent resilience against the erosive effects of time and saline waters. Our building is supported by several steel tie rods, which not only maintain the façade but also the structure, thereby resisting the replacement of the building with new architecture; the building, moreover, has stood in its location for at least two centuries. However, this begs the question: What precisely are these tie rods? After discovering Emrich's unintentional and spontaneous sculptures on a foggy night, we can imagine responding to this question in a new season once again.

A spring day following a storm reveals another facet of Venice, as the façades shimmer in the crystalline radiance brought forth by the rain. In this luminous embrace, attention is invariably drawn to the unpretentious metal adornments

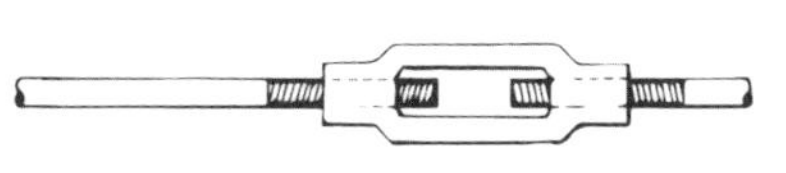

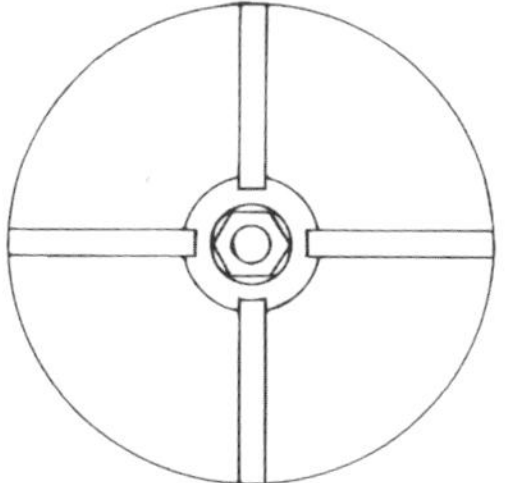

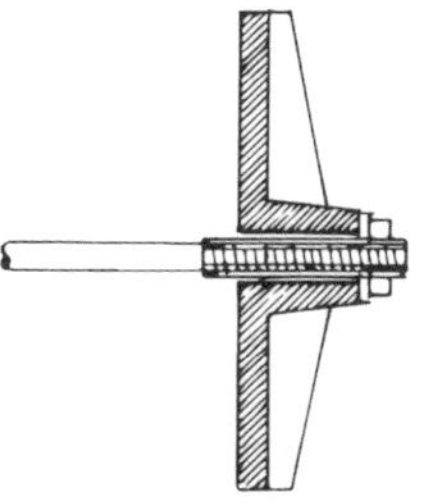

decorating nearly every palace wall. These unassuming metal bars, hooks, and large screws resembling wheel rims, often darkened or rusty, intersect with the architectural motifs of the façades, creating a tapestry of scars that bear witness to past repairs.

A closer inspection reveals them to be chains that traverse the buildings, discreetly upholding Venice's architectural edifices, fortifying them against the threat of implosion.

Originally conceived as temporary solutions, intended to await proper restoration, these chains have become an integral part of the cityscape over time, warding off the risk of collapse and alleviating the need for comprehensive refurbishments, a course of action that property owners often shy away from.[4] Remarkably, these

01

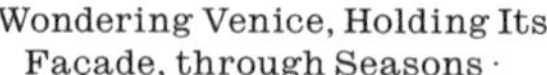

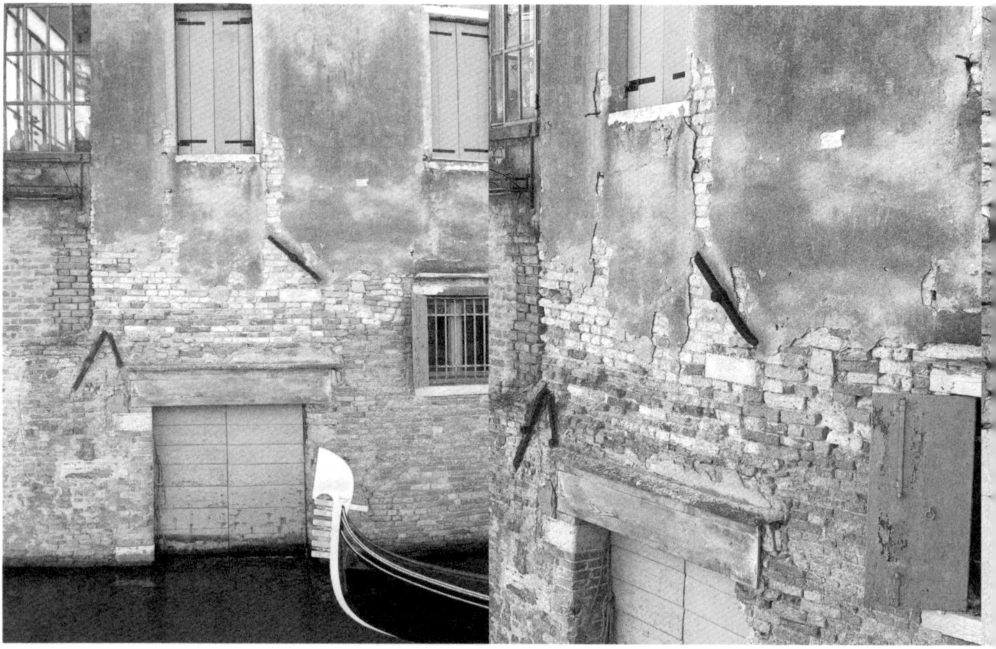

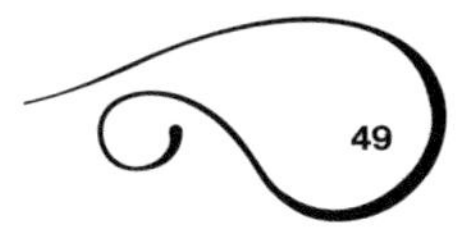

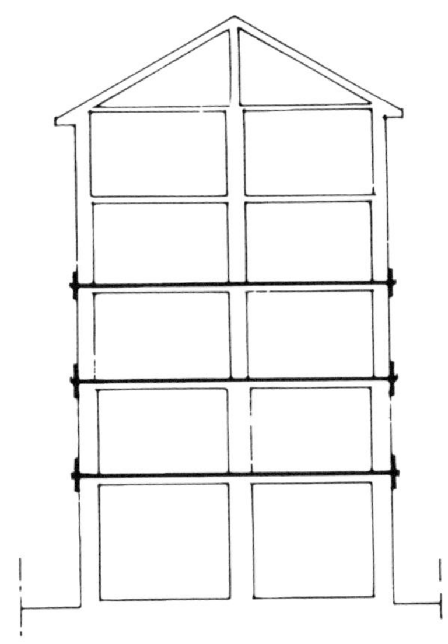

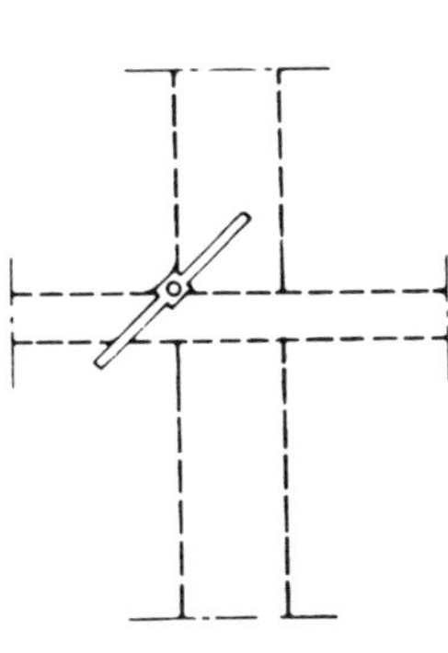

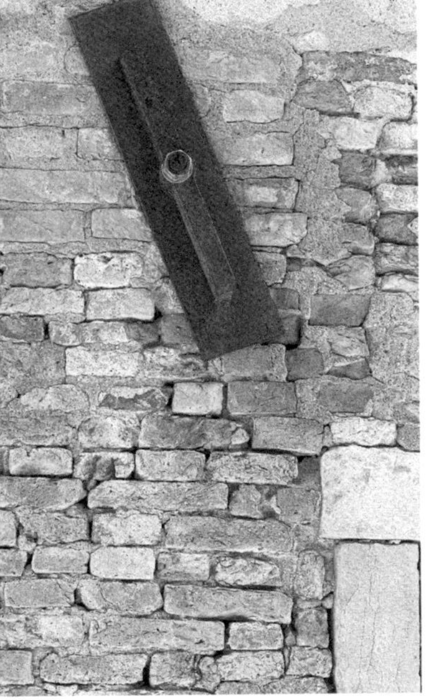

seemingly elusive elements offer invaluable insights into the structural intricacies of the city. Particularly in multistory buildings, these chains are strategically positioned at the levels of floors and beneath the pavement, thus providing an imaginative glimpse into private spaces inaccessible to us.

The façade becomes a transparent veil, and each of the chains' *capochiave* (key head) unlocks the mysteries of the invisible, unveiling a novel perspective of the city's beauty.

Massimo Cacciari, the eminent philosopher and erstwhile mayor of Venice, eloquently guides us toward understanding the city's Hellenic origins of beauty and its deep-rooted association with the built form. The Greek term *kalòn*, which constitutes the conceptual root of "beauty," alludes not merely to aesthetic allure but to the fascination with resolute strength and enduring foundation.[5] It conveys longevity, paradoxical in modern times, prompting one to question the

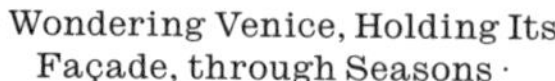

allure of beauty that renders this city both fragile yet steadfastly resilient. The imaginative force exemplified by these chains allows us to discern the life pulsating within the buildings, revealing their modes of existence as a shared symphony that we all perform through constant movement while illuminating the incessant process of stubbornly keeping these structures on Venice's unstable and marshy ground.

Finally, ending this speculative wandering within Venice by seasons, you can imagine yourself on a sweltering July day in the Piazzetta dei Leoncini under a scorching sun. Raising your gaze, you'll notice a small panel on the side wall of Palazzo Ducale depicting Alexander the Great's ascent to the sky. He is portrayed on a throne pulled by two griffins, cleverly inducing them to fly by showing them two frogs tied to lances. From such a vantage point, one wonders what the great conqueror perceives—a city that perseveres, adapts, and endures as a utopian manifestation, a monumental sculpture embodying the desire to seduce, or an unyielding pursuit of allure and permanence amid the ever-changing tides of time.

Notes

1   See the Schenk text in this
    book, p. 10-21.
2   Paolo Mauri, *Buio* (Turin:
    Einaudi, 2007), 43.
3   Alberto Savinio, *Ascolto
    il tuo cuore, città* (Milan:
    Adelphi, 2001).
4   Giuseppe Cigni, *Il consoli-
    damento murario: Tecniche
    d'intervento* (Rome:
    Edizioni Kappa, 1978).
5   Massimo Cacciari, *La città*
    (Rimini: Pazzini, 2009).

01 The chains/bars holding
    aarduork together,
    Castello 4931, Venice

On Cohesion

Marlene A. Schenk and Lena Marie Emrich

Salty Walls

Muri salati: walls from the saltwater of the sea.
While the city seems crystalline, shiny, forever
cemented into the ground and unmoving, my
body's boundaries seem to be melting, dissolving together, yet coming apart. In a book I read:
"The interweaving of time and space is briefer
and more intense in Venice than in any other city.
Moreso, it is heightened by the mirror images that
emerge, especially, from the bridges, in which the
architecture, but also the light and the shadows,
each appear in a different aggregate state: The
solid, the architecture, for a short moment becomes more fleeting, *the fleeting*, light and shad-
ow, again for a brief moment, more solid."[1]
I feel far away from myself when I walk the
streets in Venice. My body changes aggregate
states here, too; it becomes liquid, while my soul
cements itself. This does not mean that I am
becoming a part of the island, but more like I am
being swallowed by it. All things known seem
different, even the appearance of my stretched,
redefined bodily consistency.

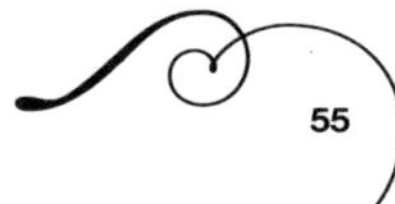

Personal Boundaries

I leave the sheltered backyard next
to Rialto Market. The eternal question
may be: How to survive within a touristic stream? Their anxiety about taking a
wrong turn is an obstacle to the collective
experience of this beautiful, ancient maze.
My right arm functions as a moving bound-
ary. I read once that the comfortable aver-
age distance between a stranger and oneself
should be sixty centimeters. In Venice,
this is an impossibility. My heart rate rises
especially on bridges. Not because of the
stairs, but because of the selfie-sticks—the
contemporary swords to claim temporary
territory to provide another image for the
digital marketplace. "What do they really
see? They heard: cries, words, echoes, but
certainly saw rather little—all the more
so their cameras saw for them." [2] #vene-
zia_non_e_disneyland. What is the value
of personal space? This may be the price a
person is willing to pay as a pedestrian in
this myth of a city.

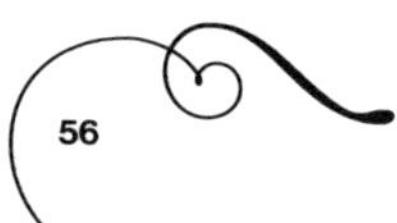

Foundation

What holds this city together is a delicate, natural construct where saltwater from the sea meets freshwater from the lagoon. Venice is built on an indirect foundation: the city itself is a sandbank, a shallow marsh on top of which sits a brick wall, embedded eighty centimeters deep in the muddy ground. Stems of oak, sometimes alder or larch, are rammed into the drained subsoil; gaps filled with clay and silt form a solid base. This construct creates a compact block called *caranto*. Wood boards are stacked over this mass topped with white Istrian limestone, *pietra d'istria*. The waterproof limestone layer forms a horizontal water barrier. Although Venice is built on 118 islands, they all stem from the same construction.

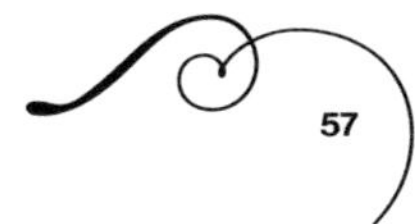

The Branch

A branch thinner than my middle finger is bent in a humble circle that takes up around a fifty- centimeter radius. Even though it seems dried out, a tension persists in its veins, resisting the forced bend. This positive resistance will soon be adapted by a stranger's hands, an artisan. I made the decision to transport the branch with my bare hands. How do you survive as a carrier of fragile goods within the clumsiness of the tourist stream? I chose the technique of uncovered fragility. There is no second skin, no shelter.

At Santa Lucia I enter the 4.2, direction: Murano. It is 10 a.m. on a mild June morning, and the boat is flooded with tourists' bodies. I hold the branch high over my head and make my way to the railing. Relief floods my body when my feet touch Murano's solid ground. The radius of my personal space expands. The well-guarded child gets delivered into the wise, graciously rough hands of the artisan. You have to relinquish control; you have to trust that he will handle the branch with the same care you gave it. Here, on this island, he will be turning it into glass, an even more fragile entity.

City as Organ

Speaking of foundations: while I change my aggregate state, the city also becomes something else. When the city breathes, it breathes heavily. It carries too much; it makes it difficult for people, builds detours. The alleys are unfathomable; they have no end, until they do, and then it's an abrupt one. The city eyes what is happening; it is in some places too cramped and almost crumbling. Its clay skeleton underwater, its joints the *campi*, as many muscles as *calli*, blood throbbing and reverberating through empty water streets. There are many one-way streets here that, actually, are not. Every one-way street contains a glimpse of another shore. Every inaccessibility leads to a detour, leads to something found that was not sought. Behind every wall, too, water from the other side sleeps noticeably against the limestone: there is always something behind the heavy, dark lung. When the city breathes, it breathes heavily but clearly.

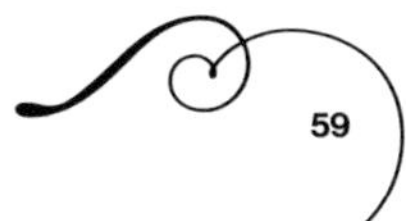

Gentle Tenderness

"Tell them I said yes" through the tender hands of the artisan.

Though I long constantly for touch, I am here only to watch. This dichotomy fills my body with a very rare excitement. Wrinkles mark wisdom and never decay on hands rough as sandpaper. Veins protrude and dissolve into a landscape of continuous blood flow circulating infinte knowledge gathered of decades. These indications leading me to the conclusion that this is the place to make the impossible possible. This shared obsession makes two worlds collide, and we become the guardians of ancient knowledge.

Curiosity seems to work as the engine, dusting off the daily routines within the traditional workshop. Our sweat runs into salty streams, reminding me of the smell of the ancient canals. It feels as if we are melting while we are merging our ideas within this liquid city.

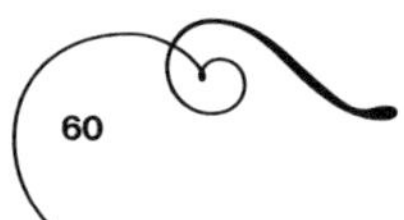

Sticky

Venice has 70,000 inhabitants when not counting the mainland; almost 30 million tourists travel to the city every year. There is a certain numbness to the touristic tide. This overload leads to an easy exit card—we drink two spritzes to get numb ourselves further, to be able to stomach it. The sugary mixture makes my fingers stick to my glass; the sun goes down. I lift the orange drink and hold it level with the water, squinting, refracting my body through all possible liquids. Venice is a city that carries extremes. Extreme dangers, extreme lightness—it is a dichotomy of perceptions. Venice is an organ that creates connections, unmanageable ones, between those seemingly unfitting singular entities. Contradictions, which work against each other at first, become partners here. None of them can do without the other.

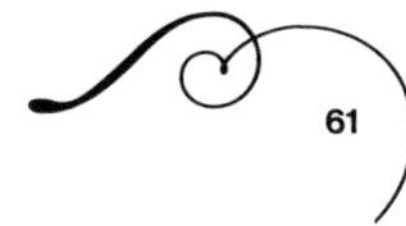

Positive Resistance

Venice has a specific smell of rotten wood and stagnant water. For me, it's a constant reminder of its resistance. A city built on wooden sticks: in some corners the smell will slap you stronger, in others it seems like you can smell the *cozze* growing. When here, the smell of rot doesn't bother me—it is a constant reminder that nothing lasts forever. The scent symbolizes the city's fragility and raises a warm melancholia in one's heart. Venetians have an untamable protective mechanism: the project MOSE (Experimental Electromechnical Module). Rows of mobile gates can isolate the Venetian lagoon temporarily from the Adriatic Sea during acqua alta. MOSE is one guardian of the city, a contemporary embodiment of a Danish mermaid sitting in the harbor. It is a shelter that, for now, can minimize the flood up to 110 centimeters and secures, for example, the Piazza San Marco. In 2025, MOSE may be able to prevent a tide of three meters from entering. The morbid smell feels cozy now.

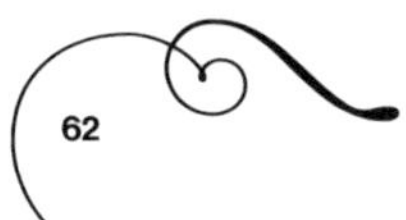

Cohesion

Like a body, any city, but especially this one, is an organism that is being held together by various facts that extend the meaning of skin.

We live in dialogues that have to be redefined again and again, like the relationship between water and land that is redetermined daily on canal walls and coastlines. As hybrid of two minds, we grow through togetherness as well as temporary rejection. We are liquifying our thoughts to create this constant powerful stream. We, too, are made out of water, like Venice; our work also has to be balanced right down to the smallest plot repeatedly, like life in a lagoon. We evaluate, stabilize, correct, always gently. "Cohesion" is a noun that applies to all these practices, the practice of our own, of the body, toward surroundings, landscapes, toward our practice of social engagement, collaborative efforts, and creative thinking. It is the sticking together that has the power to combine water and land, liquid and stone in a way that makes sense. Here is a balancing act that seems obvious. Take this hand, see the branch transform into something else. All the walls will be necessary, but all the walls will be ours: *muri unificanti.*

Notes

1   Norbert Huse, *Venedig: Von der Kunst, eine Stadt im Wasser zu bauen* (Munich: C. H. Beck, 2005), 37.

2   Michel Serres, *The Five Senses: A Philosophy of Mingled Bodies*, reprint edition (New York: Bloomsbury Academic, 2016), 86.

Marlene A. Schenk is a curator and writer.

Lena Marie Emrich is a sculptor
and multidisciplinary artist.

Mario Ciaramitaro and Alberto Restucci
are independent curators and artistic
directors of aarduork in Venice.

Pages 25 - 35

Stagnum, 2023
Melted glass on molding sand
(thermo fusion)
118 × 100 × 1 cm
Edition of 3, each unique

Near and in Fondazione
Giancarlo Ligabue

Pages 26 - 27 - 28

Pecten, 2023
Melted glass on molding sand, steel
52.5 × 52.5 × 1 cm
Edition of 3, each unique

Pages 29 - 30 - 31

Ramus, 2023
Lamp-worked borosilicate glass,
natural acrylic atone, steel
25 × 25 × 60 cm, ø 50 cm
Edition of 3, each unique

Pages 32 - 33

Fomes fomentarius, 2023
Melted glass on molding sand
(thermo fusion), steel
52.5 × 43.5 × 1 cm; 51 × 58 × 1 cm
Edition of 3, each unique

Pages 34 - 43

Algae, 2023
Melted glass on molding sand
82.5 × 70 × 1 cm
Edition of 3, each unique

In Fondazione Giancarlo Ligabue
and in a corner at Guideca

Pages 36 - 37

Succinit, 2023
Melted glass on molding sand
(thermo fusion), steel
52.5 × 52.5 × 1 cm
Edition of 3, each unique

Pages 38 - 39

Stagnum circum, 2023
Melted glass on molding sand
(thermo fusion), steel
52.5 × 52.5 × 1 cm
Edition of 3, each unique

Pages 40 - 41 - 42

Clam, 2023
Galvanized steel
90.2 × 61.5 × 61.3 cm
Edition of 2, each unique

Colophon

Thanks to the city of Venice

Thanks for the financial support

Burger COLLECTION

STIFTUNGKUNSTFONDS

Thanks to our collaboration partners
aarduork, Fondazione Giancarlo Ligabue, 6 AM glass

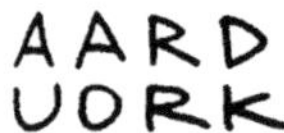

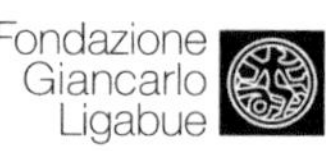

6:AM

Thanks to the heroes behind the scene
Valentina, Simone, Edoardo, Archivio di Stato Venezia, Florian,
Anne & Johanna, Jessica & Ulli, Iris & Gerhard, Andreas, Daniel & Lina, Dennis,
Conny, Marlene, Fousieh, Nadja, Anselm, Dima, Grace, Karsten, Sissi, Lorenzo,
Björn, Kitty & Hannah, Nini, Frederik, Teresa & Simone

THE DARKEST CORNERS
Marlene A. Schenk
and Lena Marie Emrich

EDITORS
Aaron Bogart
Marlene A. Schenk

COPYEDITING
Jude Macannuco

GRAPHIC DESIGN
Alice Zani

IMAGE CREDITS
Giacomo Gandolo
Marjorie Brunet-Plaza
Lena Marie Emrich

PHOTO EDITING
Valter Törsleff

PRINTER
Grafiche Antiga

TYPEFACES
Neue Haas Grotesk
Monotype Ionic Pro

PAPERS
Fedrigoni Constellation Snow
Munken Print
Fedrigoni Symbol Tatami

Printed in Crocetta del Montello, Italy

Published by
Floating Opera Press
Hasenheide 9
10967 Berlin
www.floatingoperapress.com

ISBN 978-3-9823894-7-9